91
PSALM

GOD'S UMBRELLA OF PROTECTION

Psalm 91
God's Umbrella of Protection

Copyright © 2002
Peggy Joyce Ruth BETTER LIVING Ministries
www.peggyjoyceruth.org
All rights reserved.

Printed in the United States of America

Library of Congress Control Number: 2002110752

First Printing, 2007

Cover and interior design by Garowski

Scripture quotations are from the New American Standard
Bible® (NASB) © 1960, 1977, 1995 (or from the 1977 edition)
by the Lockman Foundation. Used by permission.

07 08 09 10 11—6 5 4 3 2 1

Contents

Foreword

In the midst of these turbulent times, God has anointed Peggy Joyce to write this wonderful book, *Psalm 91: God's Umbrella of Protection.*

When someone has walked in a Truth of God for over thirty years, there is a depth of insight incomparable to anything else. Such is the case of Peggy Ruth, our dear friend and partner in the ministry. What a gift she is to the body of Christ! She is a pastor's wife, Bible teacher, radio host, and author. And there is no fluff to Peggy! She is Rock solid and has earned the right to be listened to. From her personal furnace of affliction, she has effectively explained this famous psalm and challenged us to new levels of faith and trust in God.

This is more than an inspiring book. It is a parent's manual, a leader's handbook, a pastor's promise, and a Christian's covenant. I wholeheartedly recommend this book. It contains both inspiration and information which remains biblically sound.

Along with this much needed book, Tommy and I applaud both Jack and Peggy Joyce for their unwavering faithfulness to their many assignments from the Lord. Their lives are a book!

Rachel Burchfield
President of Texas Bible Institute

Introduction

Are you tired of tormenting fear, thoughts that seem to always be lurking just below the surface, ready to control your life and steal your peace and well-being? If so, I think you will find the message in this book is the answer you've been searching for.

Maybe you fear the dangers that face your children every day—peer pressure, drugs, or alcohol. I, too, faced those fears. I also used to battle the nagging anxiety over what I would do if my husband, Jack, was in a car wreck, had a sudden heart attack, or was involved in some other tragedy that might claim his life.

Those fears that tormented my imagination used to be my constant companions. Yet it was easy to justify them with all that was going on in the world!

Back in the 1950s things were fairly predictable, but the word *predictable* became more obsolete with each passing decade. Fear ran rampant because of the uncertainty of the times—cancer, natural disasters, financial difficulties, and terrorism were everywhere I turned. But after all, didn't the Bible tell us in Luke 21:26 that in the last days, men's hearts would fail because of fear? Somehow it consoled me to know I was not alone in my dilemma.

One Sunday changed everything. That's the day the Lord miraculously, through a dream, spoke to me from a psalm I had never heard of before and answered my question, "Is there any way to be protected from all the things that are coming on the earth?" When I awoke, peace–like warm oil–flowed over me.

From that supernatural Word from God and the months of research that followed, I came to realize Psalm 91 was not merely something to bring comfort to me during times of sorrow. I saw it was there to take me victoriously through *any* crisis I might encounter.

This book is the result of the longing in my heart to help people who are struggling with the same fears I agonized over for so long. If this is something you already know, then God wants to remind you of this truth.

I encourage you to mark these Scriptures in your own Bible as we go straight through this psalm. This is God's covenant umbrella of protection for you personally.

My prayer is that Psalm 91 will give you the courage to trust.

Setting the Scene

Sundays were usually a comfort. For some reason being inside the church made the fears temporarily disappear—but not on this particular Sunday!

Our pastor looked unusually serious that day as he made the announcement that one of our most beloved and faithful deacons had been diagnosed with leukemia and had only a few weeks to live. Only the Sunday before, this robust-looking deacon in his mid-forties had been in his regular place in the choir, looking as healthy and happy as ever. Now, one Sunday later, the entire congregation was in a state of shock after hearing such an unexpected announcement.

Several of the members got upset with the pastor when he said, "Get out all of your silly little get-well cards and start sending them." I completely understood the frustration that had initiated the remark. Little did I know, however, that this incident would pave the way to a message that was going to forever burn in my heart.

Surprisingly, I had gone home from church that day feeling very little fear, perhaps because I was numb from the shock of what I had heard. I vividly remember sitting down on the edge of the bed that afternoon and saying out loud, "Lord, is there any way to be protected from all the evils that are coming on the earth?" I was not expecting an answer. I was merely voicing the thought that kept going over and over in my mind. I remember lying across the bed and immediately falling to sleep, only to wake up a short five minutes later. In those five minutes, however, I had a very unusual dream.

In the dream I was in an open field, asking the same question I had prayed earlier: "Is there any way to be protected from all the things that are coming on the earth?" And in my dream I heard these words:

> "In your day of trouble call upon
> Me, and I will answer you!"

Suddenly, I knew I had the answer I had so long been searching for. The ecstatic joy I felt was beyond anything I could ever describe. And instantly, to my surprise, there were hundreds of Christians with me in the dream out in that open field, praising and thanking God for the answer. But it wasn't until the next day, when I heard Psalm 91 referred to on a tape by Shirley Boone, that I knew in my heart that whatever was in that psalm was God's answer to my question. I nearly tore up my Bible in my haste to see what it said. And there it was in verse 15—the exact statement God had spoken to me in my dream. I could hardly believe my eyes!

I believe that you who are reading this book are

among the many Christians who were pictured with me in that open field, who will, through the message in this book, get your answer to the question, "Can a Christian be protected through these turbulent times?"

Since the early 1970s, I have had many opportunities to share this message. I believe God has commissioned me to write this book to proclaim God's Covenant of Protection. May you be sincerely blessed by it.

Peggy Joyce Ruth

Psalm 91

He who dwells in the shelter of the Most High
Will abide in the shadow of the Almighty.
I will say to the LORD, "My refuge and my fortress,
My God, in whom I trust!"
For it is He who delivers you
from the snare of the trapper
And from the deadly pestilence.
He will cover you with His pinions,
And under His wings you may seek refuge;
His faithfulness is a shield and bulwark.

You will not be afraid of the terror by night,
Or of the arrow that flies by day;
Of the pestilence that stalks in darkness,
Or of the destruction that lays waste at noon.
A thousand may fall at your side,
And ten thousand at your right hand,
But it shall not approach you.
You will only look on with your eyes
And see the recompense of the wicked.
For you have made the LORD, my refuge,
Even the Most High, your dwelling place.

No evil will befall you,
Nor will any plague come near your tent.
For He will give His angels charge concerning you,
To guard you in all your ways.
They will bear you up in their hands,
That you do not strike your foot against a stone.
You will tread upon the lion and cobra,
The young lion and the serpent
you will trample down.

"Because he has loved Me,
therefore I will deliver him;
I will set him *securely* on high,
Because he has known My name.
"He will call upon Me, and I will answer him;
I will be with him in trouble;
I will rescue him, and honor him.
"With a long life I will satisfy him
And let him behold My salvation."

1

Where Is My Dwelling Place?

He who dwells in the shelter of the Most High
Will abide in the shadow of the Almighty.
Psalm 91:1

Have you ever been inside a cabin with a big roaring fire in the fireplace, enjoying a wonderful feeling of safety and security as you watched an enormous electrical storm going on outside? It was a warm, wonderful sensation, knowing you were being sheltered and protected from the storm. That is what Psalm 91 is all about—shelter!

Did you know there is a place in God—a secret place—for those who want to seek refuge? It is a literal place of physical safety and security that God tells us about in this psalm.

Dwelling in the shelter of the Most High is the Old Testament's way of teaching faith. This gives us the most intense illustration of the very essence of personal relationship. Man has no innate, built-in shelter. Alone, he stands unsheltered against the elements and must run to THE SHELTER, which is God Himself. In the first verse of Psalm 91, God offers us more than protection; it is as if He rolls out the hospitality mat and personally invites us in.

I am sure you can think of something that represents security to you. When I think of security, shelter, and protection, I have a childhood memory that automatically comes to mind.

My parents used to take me and my younger brother and sister out on a lake near Brownwood, Texas. Dad had a secluded place where we fished for perch. That was the second greatest highlight of the outing. I loved seeing the cork begin to bob, and then, suddenly, go completely out of sight. There were only a few things that could thrill me more than jerking back on that old cane pole and landing a huge perch right in the boat. I think I was grown before I realized Dad had an ulterior motive in taking us for an afternoon of perch fishing. Those perch were his bait for the trotline he had stretched out across one of the secret coves at the lake.

Dad would drive the boat over to the place where his trotline was located, then he would cut off the boat motor and inch the boat across the cove as he "ran the trotline." That's what he called it when he would hold onto the trotline with his hands and pull the boat alongside all the strategically placed, baited hooks to see if any of them had caught a large catfish.

I said that catching the perch was the second greatest highlight of the outing. By far the greatest thrill was the times when Dad would get to a place where the trotline rope would begin to jerk almost out of his hand. It was then that we three siblings would watch, wide-eyed, as Dad wrestled with the line until finally, in victory, he flipped that huge catfish over the side of the boat, right on the floor at our feet. Money couldn't buy that kind of excitement! The circus and carnival, all rolled up into one, couldn't compete with that kind of a thrill.

One of these outings proved more eventful than most, turning out to be an experience I will never forget. It had been beautiful when we started out, but by the time we finished our perch fishing and headed toward the cove, everything had changed. A storm came up on the lake so suddenly that there was no time to get back to the boat dock. The sky turned black, lightning flashed, and drops of rain fell with such force they actually stung when they hit. Moments later, we were being pelted by marble-sized hailstones.

I saw the fear in my mother's eyes, and I knew we were in danger. But before I had time to wonder what we were going to do, Dad had driven the boat to the rugged shoreline of the only island on the lake. Boat docks surround that island now, but back then it just looked like an abandoned island with absolutely no place to take cover.

Within moments Dad had us all out of the boat and ordered the three of us to lie down beside our mother on the ground. He quickly pulled a canvas tarp out of the bottom of the boat, knelt down on the ground beside us, and thrust the tarp up over all five of us. That storm raged outside the makeshift tent he had fashioned over us; the rain beat down, the lightning flashed, and the thunder rolled. Yet I could think of nothing else but how it felt to have my dad's arms around us. There was a certain calm under the protection of the shield my father provided that is hard to explain now.

In fact, I had never felt as safe and secure in my entire life. I remember thinking I wished the storm would last forever. I didn't want anything to spoil the wonderful security I felt that day in our secret hiding place. Feeling my father's protective arms around me, I never wanted the moment to end.

Although I have never forgotten that experience, today it has taken on new meaning. Just as Dad put a tarp over us that day to shield us from the storm, our Heavenly Father has a secret place in His arms that protects us from the storms raging in the world around us.

That secret place is literal, but it is also conditional! In verse one of Psalm 91, God lists our part of the condition before He even mentions the promises included in His part. That's because our part has to come first. In order to abide in the shadow of the Almighty, we must choose to dwell in the shelter of the Most High.

The question is, how do we dwell in the security and shelter of the Most High? It is more than an intellectual experience. It is a dwelling place where we can be physically protected if we run to Him. You may utterly believe that God is your refuge, you may give mental assent to it in your prayer time, you may teach Sunday School lessons on this concept of refuge, and you may even get a warm feeling every time you think of it, but unless you do something about it-unless you actually get up and run to the shelter-you will never experience it.

You might call that place of refuge—a Love Walk! In fact, the secret place is, in reality, the intimacy and familiarity of the presence of God Himself. When our grandchildren Cullen and Meritt, ages ten and seven, stay the night with us, the moment they finish breakfast, each runs to his own secret place to spend some time talking with God. Cullen finds a place behind the couch in the family room, and Meritt heads behind the lamp table in the corner of our bedroom. Those places have become very special to them.

Where is your secret place? You too need the security and shelter of a secret place with the Most High. This place of refuge is actually a relationship with the Father you have cultivated and developed by investing enough time into it to make it very personal and intimate.

2

What Is Coming Out of My Mouth?

I will say to the LORD, "My refuge and my fortress,
My God, in whom I trust!"
Psalm 91:2

Notice that verse two above says, "I will say..." Circle the word "say" in your Bible because we must learn to verbalize our trust. We answer back to God what He says to us in the first verse. There is power in saying His Word back to Him!

We are not told to just think the Word. We are told to *say* the Word. For example, Joel 3:10 tells the weak to say, "I am a mighty man." Over and over we find great men of God such as David, Joshua, Shadrach, Meshach, and Abednego declaring their confessions of faith out loud in dangerous situations. Notice what begins to happen on the inside when you say, "Lord, You are my Refuge–You are my Fortress–You are my Lord and my God! It is in You that I put my total trust!" The more we say it out loud, the more confident we become in His protection.

So many times, as Christians, we mentally agree that the Lord is our Refuge–but that is not good enough. Power is released in saying it out loud. When we say it, and mean it, we are placing ourselves in His shelter. By voicing His Lordship and His Protection we open the door to the secret place.

One cannot miss the fact that this verse uses the word my three times: "my refuge…my fortress…my God!" The psalmist makes a personal claim to God. The reason we can trust is that we know who God is to us. This verse makes the analogy of who God is; He is a refuge and a fortress. God Himself becomes the defensive site for us against all invading enemies. He is personally our protection.

Some quote Psalm 91 as though it was some magical wand, but there is nothing magical about this psalm. It is powerful and it works simply because it is the Word of God—alive and active. And we confess it out loud simply because the Bible tells us to.

There is, however, a uniqueness about this psalm. Promises of protection can be found throughout the Bible, but Psalm 91 is the only place in the Word where all of the protection promises are brought together in one collection, forming a covenant written through the Holy Spirit. How powerful that is!

Have you ever tried to protect yourself from all the bad things that can happen? It's like trying to keep the whole law. God knows we can't do it. Psalms 60:11b tells us "…deliverance by man is in vain." God has to be our source before the promises in Psalm 91 will ever work.

We could go to the doctor once a month for a checkup. We could double-check our cars every day to see that the motor, the tires, and the brakes were all

in good running order. We could fireproof our houses and store up food for a time of need. Yet, we still
couldn't do enough to protect ourselves from every
potential danger. It's impossible!

It isn't that any one of these precautions is wrong.
It is that not one of these things, in and of itself, has
the power to protect. God has to be the One to whom
we run first. He is the only One who has an answer
for whatever might come.

> "For I know the plans that I have
> for you," declares the LORD, "plans
> for welfare and not for calamity to
> give you a future and a hope."
> (Jeremiah 29:11)

When I think of how utterly impossible it is to
protect ourselves from all the evils that are in the
world, I always think of a sheep. A sheep has no real
protection other than its shepherd. In fact, it is the
only animal I can think of that has no built-in protection. It has no sharp teeth, no offensive odor to spray
to drive off its enemies, no loud bark, and it certainly
can't run fast enough to escape danger. That's why the
Bible calls us God's sheep! God is saying, "I want you
to see Me as your source of protection. I am your
Shepherd." Now He may use doctors, storm cellars, or
bank accounts to meet our specific needs, but our

hearts have to run to Him first as our Shepherd and our Protector. Then He will choose the method He desires to bring about the protection.

When I'm facing a challenge I have learned to say, "In this particular situation of _____ (I name it out loud), I choose to trust You, Lord." The difference it makes when I proclaim my trust out loud is amazing.

Take notice of what flies out of your mouth in times of trouble. The worst thing that can happen is for something to come out that brings death. Cursing gives God nothing to work with. This psalm tells us to do just the opposite—speak life! One of those times that brought life to a death situation really stands out in my mind.

The whole family was rejoicing when our daughter-in-law, Sloan (who is pictured on the front cover with our son, Bill, and their two children, Cullen and Meritt), received a positive pregnancy test report and found that she was going to have the first grandchild on either side of the family. Since she'd had a tubal pregnancy once before that resulted in a miscarriage, making her highly susceptible for another, the doctor then ordered a sonogram as a precautionary measure.

The disturbing result of the sonogram was "no fetus found, a great deal of water in the uterus, and spots of endometriosis." With only two hours' notice, emergency surgery was quickly underway, at which time the doctor performed a laparoscopy, drained the uterus, and scraped away the endometriosis. After the surgery the doctor's words were, "During the laparoscopy we carefully looked everywhere, and there was no sign of a baby, but I want to see you back in my office in one week to be sure fluid doesn't build back up." When Sloan argued that the pregnancy test had been positive, he said there was a 99 percent chance the baby had naturally aborted and had been absorbed back into the uterine lining.

After he left the room, Sloan was the only one not fazed by the doctor's report. What she said next surprised everyone. She emphatically stated that even the doctor had left her with a 1 percent chance, and she was going to take it. From that moment, no amount of discouragement from well-meaning friends who didn't want her to be disappointed had any effect on her. Never once did she veer from confessing out loud Psalm 91 and another Scripture promise that she found: "My child will live, and not die, and declare the wonderful works of God" (Psalm 118:17). A treasured book that was very important to Sloan during this time was *Supernatural Childbirth* by Jackie Mize.

A strange look came on the technician's face the next week as she administered the ultrasound. She immediately called for the physician. Her reaction was a little disconcerting to Sloan until she heard the words, "Doctor, I think you need to come here quickly. I've just found a six-week-old fetus!" It was nothing short of a miracle that such severe, invasive procedures had not damaged or destroyed this delicate beginning stage of life. When I look at my grandson, it is hard to imagine life without him. I thank God for a daughter-in-law who believes in her covenant and is not ashamed to confess it out loud in the face of every negative report.

Our part of this protection covenant is expressed in verses one and two of Psalm 91: "he who dwells..." and "he who says…" This releases His power to bring about the promises in verses three through sixteen.

3

Two-Way Deliverance

*For it is He who delivers you from the snare of the
trapper And from the deadly pestilence.*
Psalm 91: 3

Have you ever seen a movie where a fur trapper travels deep into the mountains in the cold climate? He baits big, steel traps, covers them over with branches and then waits for some unsuspecting animal to step into the trap. Those traps were not there by chance. The trapper had taken great care in placing them in very strategic locations.

That is a picture of what the enemy does to us. That's why he is called the trapper! The traps set for us are not there by accident. It is as if your name is on it. They are custom made, placed and baited specifically for each one of us. But like an animal caught in a trap, it is a slow, painful process. You don't die instantly. You are ensnared until the trapper comes to destroy you.

The enemy knows exactly what will most likely hook us, and he knows exactly which thought to put into our minds to lure us into the trap. That is why Paul tells us in 2 Corinthians 2:11 that we are not to be ignorant of the "schemes" (traps) of the enemy. Then he says:

…for the weapons of our warfare are not of the flesh but divinely powerful for the destruction of fortresses. We *are* destroying speculations and every lofty thing raised up against the knowledge of God, and *we* are taking every thought captive to the obedience of Christ… (2 Corinthians 10:4-5)

God not only delivers us from the snare laid by the trapper (Satan), but according to the last part of verse three, He also delivers us from the deadly pestilence. I always thought a pestilence was something that attacked crops-bugs, locusts, grasshoppers, spider mites, mildew, and root rot. After doing a word study on the word pestilence, however, I found, to my surprise, that *pestilence* attacks people-not crops! A pestilence is any lethal disease.

Webster's New World Dictionary says pestilence is "any virulent or fatal disease; an epidemic that hits the masses of people-any deadly disease that attaches itself to one's body with the intent to destroy." But God says, "I will deliver you from the deadly disease that comes with the intent to destroy."

There are all kinds of enemies: temptations, spiritual enemies, and physical enemies. Initially, I was in a quandary after my word study, wondering if God really meant literal pestilence. It took me a while to see the internal workings of warfare in the body as a parallel concept with disease. Only man tries to choose between physical and spiritual deliverance; the Scripture encases both (notice how Jesus demonstrates that His power operates at all levels with a very literal, physical fulfillment in Matthew 8:16-17). When evil is served, it looks the same on the platter. Scripture deals with both through clear verses that promise physical healing and literal deliverance.

God is so good to confirm His Word when one seeks Him with an open heart. Right after I received the dream about Psalm 91 and was trying to digest all of these protection promises and comprehend the fact that God is the One who always sends good and not evil, Satan was on the other end trying to discourage my faith at every turn. Because I was very young in my conviction and struggling hard to maintain it in the midst of a world that does not believe in the supernatural goodness of God, I was devastated when a thought came into my mind one morning as I was getting ready to go to church: *If God wants us to walk in health, why did He create germs?*

That one thought was attempting to completely dismantle my faith in the newfound truth that God had provided healing in the atonement. In fact, I was so distraught I didn't even think I could motivate myself to go to church that morning. I remember I went into my bedroom and literally fell on my face before God, asking Him how those two facts could possibly be reconciled.

As clear as a bell, God spoke in my spirit: "Trust Me, get up and go, and I will give you an answer."

I got up with mixed emotions. I had unmistakably heard God speak to my spirit, but I could see no way in which He could satisfactorily resolve the question that had struck in my head. Why would God create a germ to make us sick, if He did, in fact, want us to walk in divine health? I went to church that morning under a cloud of heaviness and I couldn't tell you what subject the pastor, Bert Maxfield, preached on. But somewhere in the middle of his sermon he made this statement: "God made everything good. Take germs, for instance-germs are nothing more than microscopic plants and animals that the enemy perverted and uses to spread disease." Then he stopped, and with a strange look on his face, said, "I have no idea where that thought came from. It was not in my notes." He went right on with his sermon.

I must admit I almost disturbed the entire service because I couldn't keep from bouncing up and down on the pew. The awesomeness of God was more than I could take in without its erupting out of me. God could not have done anything that would have strengthened my faith for healing more than that incident did that morning.

Do you sometimes feel you have opposition facing you from every side? This verse is addressing the enemy's assignments from both the physical as well as the spiritual. One of our family members went to a certain country as a missionary and made the comment, "This is a country where there are numerous ways to die." Both the poor health conditions and the hostility in the country provided many dangers. There are enemies that attack your mind (thoughts), some that attack your body (germs), and some who attack you physically (people). This is your verse that insures your deliverance from all the varieties of harm.

Consider with me one more area of physical protection from harm. When Jesus sent the disciples out, He gave these instructions: "I send you out as sheep in the midst of wolves; so be shrewd as serpents and innocent as doves" (Matthew 10:16). It is an interesting piece of instruction to be told to have the cleverness of a snake (in order not to be harmed) but the innocence of a dove (in order not to cause harm).

Each year at the Texas Rattlesnake Roundup, men often disassemble rattlesnakes with their knives for the gaping audience. Before milking the snake of its poison, they slice open the thick, scaly skin covering with its agile muscular structure and pry open the snake's mouth to reveal the fangs. After seeing the internal workings, it becomes obvious that the snake is geared for causing harm. Not so with the dove. When a hunter cleans a dove, first he pulls off the feathers. There are no thick scales, no dangerous claws, no poisonous venom. The dove has nothing in him that causes harm.

In Christ's analogy we are advised as sheep among wolves to be as clever as the snake, but as innocent as the dove. This takes care of harm in two directions. I believe you can claim the promise of this verse-for God to protect you from being harmed and from your harming innocent people. Pray, for example, that God protects you from ever hitting a child on a bicycle, being involved in a wreck that kills another person, or causing someone to walk away from the faith. Many a person has been traumatized from inadvertently hurting someone he never intended to hurt. God has this preventive promise in verse three for us to stand on for protection from both ways in which harm can destroy a life.

In the same way, notice the twofold aspect to this deliverance in verse three: from the snare of the trapper and from the deadly pestilence. This covers being delivered from temptation and being delivered from harm. It is similar to the request in the Lord's Prayer: "Do not lead us into temptation, but deliver us from evil" (Matthew 6:13). What good would it do to be delivered from harm-only to be caught in a sin that destroys us? On the other hand, what good would it do to be delivered from a sin-only to be destroyed by a deadly pestilence? This verse covers both. Thank God for His deliverance from both traps and pestilence.

4

Under His Wings

He will cover you with His pinions,
And under His wings, you may seek refuge.
Psalm 91:4a

When you picture a magnificent flying bird, it is usually not a chicken that comes to mind. I've never seen a chicken portrayed in flight-many eagles, but no chickens. We quote the Scripture from Isaiah 40:31 that talks about being borne up on the wings of eagles or with wings like eagles. There is a difference, however, between being "on" His wings and being "under" His wings. This promise in Psalm 91 is not elaborating on the flying wing but on the sheltering wing. One indicates strength and accomplishment, while the other denotes protection and familiarity. When you imagine the warmth of a nest and the security of being under the wings of the nurturing love of a mother hen with chicks, it paints a vivid picture of the sheltering wing of God's protection that the psalmist refers to in this passage.

Is everyone protected under the wings? Did you notice it says He will cover you with His pinions (feathers), and under His wings, you *may* seek refuge? Again, it's up to us to make that decision! We can seek refuge under His wings if we *choose* to.

The Lord gave me a vivid picture of what it

means to seek refuge under His wings. My husband, Jack, and I live out in the country, and one spring our old mother hen hatched a brood of baby chickens. One afternoon when they were scattered all over the yard, I suddenly saw the shadow of a hawk overhead. I then noticed something that taught me a lesson I will never forget. That mother hen did not run to those little chicks and jump on top of them to try to cover them with her wings. No!

Instead, she squatted down, spread out her wings, and began to cluck. And those little chickens, from every direction, came running to her to get under those outstretched wings. Then the hen pulled her wings down tight, tucking every little chick safely under her. To get to those babies, the hawk would have to go through the mother.

When I think of those baby chicks running to their mother, I realize it is under His (God's) wings where we may seek refuge-but we have to run to Him. "He will cover you with His pinions, and under His wings, you may seek refuge." That one little word, may, is a strong word! It is up to us. All that mother hen did was cluck and expand her wings to tell them where to come.

Oh, Jerusalem, Jerusalem…How often I wanted to gather your children together, the way a hen gath-

ers her chicks under her wings,
and you were unwilling. (Matthew
23: 37)

Notice the contrast between God's willingness and our unwillingness—His "wanting" against our "not wanting to"-His "would" against our "would not." What an amazing analogy to show us that there is protection offered that we don't accept!

It is interesting that Jesus uses the correlation of maternal love to demonstrate His attachment to us. There is a certain fierceness to motherly love we cannot overlook. God is deeply committed to us—yet at the same time, we can reject His outstretched arms if we so choose. It is available, but not automatic. God does not run here and there, trying to cover us. He said, "I have made protection possible. You run to Me!" And when we do run to Him in faith, the enemy will have to go through God to get to us. What a comforting thought!

5

A Mighty Fortress Is My God

His faithfulness is a shield and bulwark.
Psalm 91:4b

It is God's faithfulness to His promises that is our shield. It is not solely *our* faithfulness! God will be faithful to the promises He has made.

When the enemy comes to whisper fearful or condemning thoughts in your mind, you can ward off his attack by saying, "My faith is strong because I know my God is faithful, and His faithfulness is my shield!"

How often I've heard people say, "I can't dwell in the shelter of God. I mess up and fall short too many times. I feel guilty and unworthy." God knows all about our weaknesses. That's why He gave His Son. We can no more earn this protection, or deserve it, than we can earn or deserve our salvation. The main thing is that if we slip and fall, we must not stay down. Get up, repent, and get back under that shield of protection. Thankfully this verse says it is His faithfulness, not ours, that is our shield.

> If we are faithless, He remains faithful, for He cannot deny Himself. (2 Timothy 2:13)

Don't point to what you've done or haven't done. Point to what Jesus has done for you. We dwell in His shelter by faith in God's grace (see Ephesians 2:8-9). And faith is not hard. It is simply our response to what Jesus has already provided through His blood. We cannot perform enough good deeds to keep ourselves in His shelter anymore than we can do enough to keep ourselves saved. We have to realize we dwell in His shelter—not in our own righteousness but in the righteousness of Jesus Christ.

> But by His doing you are in Christ Jesus, who became to us wisdom from God, and righteousness... (1 Corinthians 1:30)

There is a difference, however, between making an occasional mistake and staying in willful sin. Self-will and rebellion will keep us out of the secret place of protection because self-will is a wall we build between God and us.

My daughter once slipped and fell facedown in the busiest four-way intersection in our city. Embarrassment made her want to keep lying there so she didn't have to look up and show her face to so many people who would know her in a small town. Yet the worst thing she could have done was to lie there in that heavy traffic area. This is a humorous illustration of what it looks like when we fall spiritually. When you think of my daughter lying facedown in the middle of the street, don't ever forget that the worst thing you can do after you fall spiritually is fail to get up!

Psalm 91:4b expresses again God's commitment and faithfulness to being our shield of protection. It is His faithfulness that gets us back on our feet and moving again. His unshakable faithfulness is a literal shield. I have this awesome mental picture of a huge shield in front of me, completely hiding me from the enemy. The shield is God Himself. His faithfulness to His promises guarantees us that His shield will remain forever steadfast and available. Whether or not we stay behind the protection of that shield is our choice.

Sometimes we have no power to rescue ourselves and we have to rely solely on His faithfulness. I saw this illustrated during one of the floods we had in our town several years ago. Our twenty-year-old son, Bill, had a flock of goats on some land by the bayou. As the bayou water began to rise and overflow its banks, some men saw Bill's goats being overtaken by the flood. They hoisted the goats up into the loft of a barn to keep them from drowning. By the next morning the water was like a rushing river—a mile wide—washing away uprooted trees and everything else in its path. Bill had, by this time, been told about his goats, so in spite of the roadblocks and the rapids gushing by, he set out in an old tin-bottom boat across those swift floodwaters to rescue his little flock. He knew that in another few hours they would die from thirst and suffocation.

Little Willie was the most precious of all the herd because of the time Bill had spent bottle–feeding him. The cry of that little goat was the first Bill heard when he got close to the barn. And as you might expect, once Bill forced the loft door open amid the rushing waters, Little Willie was the first to jump into his arms. Then, boatload by boatload, goat by goat, Bill was able to get every one of those animals out of the loft and row them to safety.

A television camera crew from Abilene, while filming the flood, caught sight of the goat boy risking his life to rescue his goats. That was the news story of the day, making the broadcast at six o'clock and again at ten. It was a heartwarming story, but every time I think of Bill rescuing those goats in trouble, I think of how God sees us in our troubles and finds ways to rescue us.

Bill had to risk his own life to save Little Willie when the goat had no means of rescuing himself. This reminds me of the verse where Jesus talks about the times a shepherd must leave everything to go after the one sheep that needs help-which is, in fact, the Gospel in a nutshell. The shepherd lifts that sheep onto his shoulder and carries him back to safety. In the same way, God's faithfulness reaches us in our deepest moment of need.

Psalm 91:4b also tells us that God's faithfulness is our bulwark. According to *Nelson's Bible Dictionary*, "a bulwark is a tower built along a city wall from which defenders shoot arrows and hurl large stones at the enemy." Think about that!

From that tower, God is faithful to point out the enemy so he can't sneak up on our blind side. Note that this verse declares God's faithfulness to us as both a shield and a bulwark in a two-layered analogy. The passage uses two images of fortification and protection. God is our tower—our wall of protection in a collective sense; and He is our shield—a very personal and individualized defense. This verse indicates *double* protection.

6

I Will Not Fear the Terror

You will not be afraid of the terror by night...
Psalm 91:5a

It is interesting to note that verses five and six of Psalm 91 cover an entire twenty-four-hour period, emphasizing day-and-night protection. But what is more important is that these two verses encompass every evil known to man.

The psalmist divides the list into four categories. We will look at those categories one at a time, chapter by chapter. The first–terror by night–includes all the evils that come through man: kidnapping, robbery, rape, murder, terrorism, wars. It is the dread–or horror–or alarm–that comes from what man can do to you. God is saying, "You will not be afraid of any of those things...because they will not approach you." The first thing verse five deals with is fear.

Never before in our history has there been so much talk of terrorism and germ warfare, but to the surprise of so many people, God is not shocked or caught off guard by these things. Do we think chemical warfare is bigger than God?

Long before man ever discovered biological weapons, God made provision for the protection of His people-if they would believe His Word.

> "These signs will accompany those
> who have believed…if they drink
> any deadly *poison,* it will not hurt
> them. (Mark 16:17-18)

According to the *Strong's Concordance,* the word *drink* in this Scripture comes from the Greek word which means "to drink, to absorb, to inhale, or to take into the mind." No evil has been conceived by man against which God has not provided a promise of protection for any of His children who will choose to believe it and act on it.

What about the fear that has come on mankind regarding our polluted water supplies, foods contaminated by pesticides? I believe the Word of God advocates using wisdom, but all the precautions in the world cannot protect us from every harmful thing that could be in our food and water. Therefore, God's instruction to bless our food and water before eating is not merely some ritual to make us look more spiritual. Rather, it is another provision for our safety, playing an important role in God's protective plan.

> But the Spirit explicitly says that in
> later times…men…[will] advocate
> abstaining from foods which God
> has created to be gratefully shared
> in by those who believe and know

the truth. For everything created by God is good, and nothing is to be rejected if it is received with gratitude; for it is sanctified by means of the word of God and prayer. (1 Timothy 4:1-5)

"But you shall serve the LORD your God, and He will bless your bread and your water; and I will remove sickness from your midst." (Exodus 23:25)

It is the goodness of God that He made provision before we ever asked! This is not for everyone; it is for those who believe and know the truth. Blessing the food with gratitude literally brings about sanctification–a cleansing of our food and water.

Over and over Jesus told us, "Do not fear!" Why do you think He continually reminds us not to be afraid? Because it is through faith in His Word that we are protected-and since fear is the opposite of faith, the Lord knows fear will keep us from operating in the faith that is necessary to receive. It is no wonder God addresses the fear of terror first.

So how do we keep from being afraid? It's very simple! Fear comes when we think we are responsible for bringing about this protection ourselves. Too often we think, *Oh, if I can just believe hard enough, maybe I'll be protected.* That's wrong thinking. The protection is already there. It has already been provided, whether we receive it or not. Faith is simply the choice to receive what Jesus has already done. The Bible has classic examples of how to deal with fear.

The answer is in the blood of Jesus. Exodus 12:23 tells us when Israel put blood on the door facings, the destroyer could not come in. The animal blood they used then serves as a type and shadow, or a picture, of the blood of Jesus which ratifies our better protection—under our better covenant.

When we confess out loud, "I am protected by the blood of Jesus," and believe it, the devil literally cannot come in. Remember, verse two tells us, "I will say to the LORD, my refuge and my fortress." It is heart and mouth-believing with our heart and confessing with our mouth.

Our physical weapons are operated with our hands, but we operate our spiritual weapons with our mouths. The blood is applied by saying it in faith. Confessing with our mouth and believing with our heart starts with the new birth experience and sets precedence for receiving all of God's good gifts (see Romans 10:9-10).

If we find ourselves afraid of the terror by night, that is our barometer to let us know we are not dwelling and abiding up close to the Lord in the shelter of the Most High and believing His promises. Fear comes in when we are confessing things other than what God has said. When our eyes are not on God, fear will come. But let that fear be a reminder to repent.

> We walk by faith, not by sight.
> (2 Corinthians 5:7)

We have to choose to believe His Word more than we believe what we see—more than we believe the terror attack. Not that we deny the existence of the attack. The attack may be very real, but God wants our faith in His Word to become more of a reality to us than what we see in the natural.

For example: gravity is a fact. No one denies the existence of gravity, but just as the law of aerodynamics can supersede the law of gravity, Satan's attacks can also be superseded by a higher law-the law of faith and obedience to God's Word. Faith does not deny the existence of terror. There are simply higher laws in the Bible for overcoming it.

David did not deny the existence of the giant. Fear has us compare the size of the giant to ourselves. Faith, on the other hand, had David compare the size of the giant to the size of his God. David's eyes saw the giant, but his faith saw the promises (see 1 Samuel 17).

Our daughter had a friend, Julee, living in an apartment in Fort Worth, Texas. She was getting ready for church one Sunday morning when someone knocked on her door. Never dreaming it wasn't someone she knew, she opened the door, only to be almost knocked over by a strange man who shoved his way in and attacked her.

Julee started using the Word of God as her defense. In the natural there was no way for a young girl to escape from a strong man, but confidence in her God allowed her not to give up!

It took forty-five minutes of spiritual battle as he came at her time after time. But her persistence in quoting these words out of Psalm 91 brought confusion and immobility on him, thwarting every attempted attack. And during one of those times when he was at a standstill, she was able to get out the door and escape unharmed.

Later, after he was apprehended and held in custody, she found he had sexually assaulted numerous young women, and she was the only one of his victims who had been able to escape without harm. We do not have to be afraid of the terror of what man can do to harm us. Praise God for our higher law! God's laws triumph over man's laws.

7

I Will Not Fear the Arrow

You will not be afraid of...the arrow that flies by day.
Psalm 91:5

The second category of evil is the arrow that flies by day. An arrow is something that pierces or wounds spiritually, physically, mentally, or emotionally. This category indicates that you are in a spiritual battle zone; specific enemy assignments are directed toward your life to defeat you.

Arrows are deliberately sent by the enemy and meticulously aimed at the spot that will cause the most damage. They are targeted toward the area where our mind is not renewed by the Word of God-perhaps an area where we are still losing our temper or where we are still easily offended–or perhaps, an area of rebellion or fear!

Seldom does the enemy attack us in an area where we are built up and strong. He attacks us where we're still struggling. That's why we have to run to God! And when we do battle using our spiritual weapons, the enemy's arrows will not approach us.

God tells us in Ephesians 6:16 that we have a "shield of faith" to extinguish all the flaming darts of the enemy. Arrows indicate intentional danger. Someone has to bend the bow and pull back the bow string. The arrows are aimed and released. These are not just regular, everyday arrows; they are on fire. Yet God doesn't say we can miss *most* of them. He says that we can extinguish *all* of them. When arrows are sent to wound us spiritually, physically, emotionally, or financially, God wants us to ask and believe by faith that He will pick us up and deliver us from calamity.

Long before my husband and I moved full-time into ministry, we owned and operated a soft drink bottling plant that his dad had started the year before Jack was born. Several years before we sold the business, one of the other bottling plants in our area changed management, and the new manager told us he was going to spare no expense in putting us out of business.

He told the truth! We could never have anticipated how much money he was going to spend trying to fulfill his promise. He literally went all over town, placing free vending machines wherever our venders were located. Storeowners were continually calling us to come and pick up our equipment. Financially, there was no way to compete, especially when the manager also started product price-cutting and flooding the market with advertising. The outlook in the natural was pretty dismal, but we had something he didn't have. We had a covenant with God, telling us not to be afraid of the arrow that flies by day.

And God is faithful. Those arrows–or circumstances–that had looked impossible for us to overcome finally passed, and our business was left standing long after the competition was gone. The competitor had obviously expected our business to fold quickly under the intense financial pressure, but when we were able to survive longer than he anticipated, it was he who went under financially.

We have a covenant with God telling us not to be afraid of the arrow that flies by day. Assignments will rise up, but don't be afraid. He has promised to protect us and He has promised the arrows will not hit their target.

8

I Will Not Be Afraid of the Pestilence

You will not be afraid...
Of the pestilence that stalks in darkness.
Psalm 91:5-6a

Fear gripped my heart and beads of perspiration popped out on my forehead as I feverishly ran my fingers over what felt like a lump in my body. How I dreaded that monthly self-examination the doctor had suggested. My fingertips were as cold as ice from the panic I had worked up just thinking about what I might find, and the turn my life would take from there.

On that particular day it turned out to be a false alarm, but the dread of what I might find in the coming months was constantly in the back of my mind until this promise came alive in my heart. If you fight fears of fatal diseases, then this is the Scripture for you to take hold of.

The third category of evil that God names is *pestilence*. This is the only evil He names twice! Since God doesn't waste words, He must have a specific reason for repeating this promise.

Have you noticed when a person says something more than once, it is usually because he wants to emphasize a point? God knew the pestilence and the fear that would be running rampant in these end days.

The world is teeming with fatal epidemics that are hitting people by the thousands, so God catches our attention by repeating this promise.

It's as though God is saying, "I said it in verse three, but did you really hear Me? Just to be sure, I am saying it again in verse six-you do not have to be afraid of the deadly pestilence!" This is so contrary to the world in which we live that we have to renew our thinking before we can comprehend the fact we do not have to be afraid of the sicknesses and diseases that are epidemic in the world today.

When I first started studying this psalm, I remember thinking, *I don't know whether I have the faith to believe these promises.* This thought stretched my faith and my mind until I thought it would snap like a rubber band that was being pulled too tightly.

God, however, reminded me that faith is not a feeling. Faith is simply choosing to believe what He says in His Word. The more I chose to believe God's Word, the more I had a knowing I could trust and rely on it completely.

> "Heaven and earth will pass away,
> but My words will not pass away."
> (Mark 13:31)

Our inheritance is not limited to what is handed down to us genetically from our ancestors. Our inheritance can be what Jesus provided for us if we believe the Word and put it to work.

> Christ redeemed us from the curse
> of the Law, having become a curse
> for us… (Galatians 3:13)

The pestilence mentioned here in Psalm 91 is spelled out in detail in Deuteronomy 28. The Scripture in Galatians tells us we are redeemed from every curse (including pestilence) if we will simply believe and appropriate the promise.

In Bible days when they mentioned pestilence, they were thinking of diseases like leprosy. Luke 21:11 states that among the signs of the end times is an outbreak of pestilence. And today we have many widespread diseases such as AIDS, cancer, and heart disease. But no matter what pestilence we might be facing, His promise never ceases to be true. The enemy may try to cause sudden surprises to catch us unaware and knock us down, but God is faithful. His Word is true no matter what the circumstances look like. I shudder to think what we might open ourselves up to without the promise of Psalm 91 and without the determination to stand firm and refuse to entertain fearful thoughts.

I wish I had kept a diary through the years of the healing miracles I have seen personally. I remember the night our son was born and we were told he had a lung disease and could not be taken out of the incubator, even to be fed. After we got over the initial shock, God seemed to just drop faith in our hearts and there was never another question in our minds whether or not he would be normal. Two perfectly healthy lungs demonstrated God's healing power.

I remember when Mary Ann Ross, with three incurable diseases, was practically carried into one of my Bible study meetings and laid on the couch. Her little eighty-seven-pound body looked to be beyond hope, but the group prayers that morning incited a miracle and twenty years later she lives. She often shows the picture on her old driver's license to illustrate the shocking difference.

I remember the night that a member of the staff at the Texas Youth Commission approached my husband and daughter. He had been listening to their Bible studies each Monday night and wanted prayer. Two tests showed his unborn child to have Down's syndrome, but he and his wife had chosen against the recommendation to have the baby aborted and just wanted Jack and Angie to pray for them as parents. Instead, they asked if they could pray that God would bring forth a miracle. Several months later his wife gave birth to a completely whole and healthy baby. Time and space prevents my sharing all the wonderful miracles I have witnessed through the years-some instantaneous, some through a miracle process, but all brought about by the hand of God.

What we allow our mind to dwell on is our choice. Therefore, if we desire to operate in this protection covenant, taking authority over negative thoughts and emotions is imperative. It is amazing how the simple phrase, "I am just not going there," will dispel those fears immediately.

I'm sure this Psalm 91 promise of protection from plagues and pestilence reminded the Jews of Israel's complete immunity from the Egyptian plagues in the land of Goshen. The destroyer could not come in where the blood was applied. The Bible claims that over one million people in the wilderness did not get sick. Even without the completed work on the cross, the Old Testament covenant has declared, "You will not be afraid of the pestilence that stalks in darkness-it will not approach you."

9

I Will Not Fear the Destruction

You will not be afraid of...the destruction
that lays waste at noon.
Psalm 91:5-6b

This fourth category of evil is destruction. Destruction takes in the evils over which mankind has no control—those things that the world ignorantly calls acts of God: tornadoes, floods, hurricanes, fire. God very plainly tells us that we are not to fear destruction. These natural disasters are not coming from God.

In Mark 4:39, Jesus rebuked the storm and it became perfectly calm, demonstrating that God is not the author of such things—otherwise, Jesus would never have contradicted His Father by rebuking something sent by Him.

There is no place in the world you can go and be safe from every destruction, every natural disaster. We can never anticipate what might come when we least expect it. But no matter where you are in the world, God says to run to His shelter where you will not be afraid of the destruction...it will not approach you!

Late one night, soon after building our new home in the country, our family was faced with a severe weather alert. The local radio station warned that a tornado had been sited just south of the country club—the exact location of our property. We could see several of the React Club vehicles parked on the road below our hill as the members watched the funnel cloud that seemed to be headed straight for our house.

I had never seen such a strange, abnormal color in the night sky or experienced such a deafening silence in the atmosphere. You could literally feel the hair on your body stand on end. Some of our son's friends were visiting, and to their surprise, Jack quickly ordered our family to get outside with our Bibles and start circling the house-reading Psalm 91 and taking authority. Jack had the children out speaking directly to the storm, just like Jesus did.

The eerie silence suddenly turned into a roar, with torrents of rain coming down in what seemed like bucketsful. Finally, Jack got a peace that the danger had passed, even though by sight nothing had changed.

We walked back into the house just in time to hear the on-location radio announcer exclaim with so much excitement that he was almost shouting, "This is nothing short of a miracle-the funnel cloud south of the Brownwood Country Club has suddenly lifted back in the sky and vanished before our very eyes."

You should have seen those kids jumping and hollering. It was the first time my son's friends had observed the supernatural at work. Their surprise, however, was no greater than that of my daughter's college professor the next day. He asked the students in his class what they were doing during the storm. Several said that they were in the bathtub under a mattress. Some were in closets and one was in a storm cellar.

You can imagine the astonishment when he got around to our daughter, Angelia, who said, "With the tornado headed our direction, my family was circling the house, quoting from Psalm 91: 'We will not be afraid of the destruction that lays waste…it will not approach us.'"

Did you know that *every* extreme evil known to man will fall into one of these four categories that we have named in chapters six through nine: *terror, arrows, pestilence,* and *destruction?* And the amazing thing is that God has offered us deliverance from them all!

God lets us know in Psalm 91, "You will not be afraid of terror, arrows, pestilence, or destruction because I have said in My Word that it will not approach you–if you are obedient to dwell in My shelter and abide in My shadow." And of course, we cannot dwell and abide in Him apart from Jesus. But praise God!–because of the shed blood of the Cross, it has now been made possible.

We can receive anything that God has already provided. The secret is knowing that everything for which God has made provision is clearly spelled out and defined in the Word of God. If you can find where God has offered it, you can have it! It is never God holding it back. His provision is already there, waiting to be received.

Faith is not a tool to manipulate God into giving you something you want. Faith is simply the means by which we accept what God has already made available. Our goal needs to be the renewal of our minds, to such an extent that we have more faith in God's Word than in what we see. God does not make promises that are out of our reach.

When the Lord first began showing me these promises and my mind was struggling with doubt, He took me to a portion of His Word that helped to set me free.

> What then? If some did not believe, their unbelief will not nullify the faithfulness of God, will it? May it never be! Rather, let God be found true, though every man *be found* a liar, as it is written, "THAT YOU MAY BE JUSTIFIED IN YOUR WORDS, AND PREVAIL WHEN YOU ARE JUDGED."
> (Romans 3:3-4)

God is telling us that even though there may be some who don't believe, their unbelief will never nullify His promises to the ones who do believe. A very important part of that verse in Romans 3 is the reminder, in a quote from the Old Testament, that what we as individuals choose to believe and confess will determine our own individual judgment.

Without the promises of protection throughout the Word of God, and especially, without our Psalm 91 covenant-listing all of the protection promises in one chapter-we might feel rather presumptuous if, on our own, we asked God to protect us from all the things covered in these four categories. In fact, we probably would not have the nerve to ask for all of that, but God is so good. He offered this protection to us before we even had a chance to ask! It was God's plan to provide protection for His children, even before the foundation of the world.

10

Though a Thousand Fall…

A thousand may fall at your side
And ten thousand at your right hand,
But it shall not approach you.
Psalm 91:7

Do we ever stop to consider what God is saying to us in verse seven? Do we have the courage to trust God's Word enough to believe that He means this literally? Is it possible for this to be true and for us to miss out on the promise?

Jesus answers the last question in Luke 4:27: "There were many lepers in Israel in the time of Elisha the prophet; and none of them was cleansed." Only Naaman the Syrian was healed when he obeyed in faith. Not everyone will receive the benefits of this promise in Psalm 91. Only those who believe God and hold fast to His promises will profit; nonetheless, it is available. And to the measure we trust Him, we will in the same measure reap the benefits of that trust.

What an awesome statement! God wants us to know that even though there will be a thousand falling by our side and ten thousand at our right hand, it does not negate the promise that destruction will not approach the one who chooses to believe and trust His Word. *The Amplified Bible* says, "…it shall not approach you *for any purpose*" (emphasis added). He means exactly what He says.

It is no accident that this little statement is tucked right here in the middle of the psalm. Have you noticed how easy it is to become fearful when disaster strikes all around you? We begin to feel like Peter must have felt as he walked on the water to Jesus. It is easy to see how he started sinking into the waves when he saw all the turbulence of the storm going on around him.

God knew there would be times when we would hear so many negative reports, see so many needs, and encounter so much danger around us that we would feel overwhelmed. That is why He warned us ahead of time that thousands would be falling all around us. He didn't want us to be caught off guard. But at that point, we have a choice to make. The ball is then in our court! We can either choose to run to His shelter in faith and it will not approach us or we can passively live our lives the way the world does, not realizing there is something we can do about it.

What tremendous insight, after our minds have been renewed by the Word of God, to realize, contrary to the world's thinking, that we do not have to be among the ten thousand who fall at our right hand.

Psalm 91 is the preventive measure that God has given to His children against every evil known to mankind. No place else in the Word are all of the protection promises (including help from angels, as well as promises insuring our authority) accumulated in one covenant to offer such a total package for living in this world. It is both an offensive and defensive measure to ward off every evil before it has had time to strike. This is not only a cure, but a plan for complete prevention!

A year after Hurricane Ivan hit, Jack and I stayed in the beach home of our friends John and Virginia Loyd in Orange Beach, Alabama. For one week we just drove through the area, appalled at the devastation we saw even after that many months of repairs had taken place. A stone's throw from their house, all the decking at the public boat docks, the gigantic dry dock building, and the restaurant glass had all been blown away. What was left of the marina building was under three feet of water. On the other side of the house, we could see what once was a shopping center had been reduced to a pile of rubble. Condos and hotels were completely gutted. Even after that length of time, mounds of siding and roofing shingles from the houses next to our friends' beach home still littered the adjacent properties.

Only after seeing the destruction with our own eyes did we realize the supernatural protection the Loyds had received. Prior to and during the hurricane, they had called us often, stating their total trust in the Lord's Psalm 91 covenant promise of protection and getting us to join in faith with them. When they returned to the area there was NO damage to their beach house or property. When a hurricane passes over, flooding brings much of the destruction because the water goes everywhere. Only God knows how He kept the water out of their beach home. THE WORD WORKS!

Did I mention that at the time the Loyds also owned a beachfront condo just three blocks away that was up for sale? In spite of the fact that the condo was directly on the ocean, when John opened the door to the condo not even a picture on the wall had been disturbed, nor was the patio glass broken. Yet the eye of Hurricane Ivan had gone directly over the top of their building. Coincidence? If you had driven down Beach Road (even a year later, when we did) you would know that it was nothing but the power of God that protected them. Praise God! Psalm 91 is not limited to areas where hurricanes can't reach. We can even be immune in the midst of mass destruction.

> You will only look on with your eyes And see the recompense of the wicked. (Psalm 91:8)

You will see recompense (payment) being doled out at times. There *is* judgment. Every sin will be exposed sooner or later and paid for. An evil dictator falls, an unrighteous aggressor is stopped, a tyrant faces his crimes against humanity, a wrong is rectified—the recompense of the wicked speaks of justice. Wars have been fought where one side had a righteous cause, and consequently, good won over evil. The justness of God is that evil will not triumph—that Hitlers do not win—that communistic governments fall—that darkness does not extinguish light.

This verse says that we will "only look on" and see it happening. The word *only* denotes a protection of only seeing and not experiencing the evil; and it denotes detachment in that the evil we see does not get inside of us. We are set apart in that we do not allow our enemy's hate to change us.

Let's look for just a moment at this Scripture with our faith in mind. Do we sometimes fall short into unbelief? Faith in God, in His Son Jesus Christ, and in His Word is counted in God's eyes as righteousness. But when we are in unbelief, to a degree we are placing ourselves in the category of the wicked. Sometimes, even as a Christian, I have been an unbelieving believer when it comes to receiving all of God's Word.

Jesus says in Matthew 5:18, "Not the smallest letter or stroke shall pass from the Law until all is accomplished." Even if believers have never utilized this psalm in its full potential, the truth has never passed away or lost one ounce of its power.

Many people think of the gospel as an insurance policy, securing only their eternity and their comfort after disaster strikes. They are depriving themselves of so much. Perhaps we all need to ask ourselves the question, "What kind of coverage do I have-fire or life?" God's Word is more than just an escape from hell; it is a handbook for living a victorious life in this world.

There is a difference between the destruction of the enemy and persecution for the gospel's sake. Paul writes in 2 Timothy 3:12, "All who desire to live godly in Christ Jesus will be persecuted." There are times when we will be mistreated because of our stand for the cause of Christ. But Psalm 91 is not dealing with persecution. Jesus suffered persecution, but He did not face calamity, disaster, and mishap. Accidents never even approached Him.

> A thousand may fall at your side
> And ten thousand at your right hand,
> But it shall not approach you...For you have made the LORD, my refuge,
> Even the Most High, your dwelling place. (Psalm 91:7-9)

Have you ever been in spiritual warfare where it

seemed that everyone was falling around you? If this verse isn't a description of actual combat, I don't know what is-and yet, tied to it is a promise of protection beyond anything that can be envisioned. There is a place where calamity literally does not even approach us. This concept is hard to imagine in a peaceful season of life, yet how much more remarkable is this promise when it's given in connection with the spiritual battle described above. The portrayal of people falling is directly connected to the promise that it will not even come near us. Two opposite poles joined together! This psalm is making its strongest offer of protection right in the midst of chaos. And it is a type of protection that stands in a category all its own.

Too many people see Psalm 91 as a beautiful promise that they file right alongside all of their other quality reading material. It makes them feel comforted every time they read it. But I do not want anyone to read this book and fail to see the superior significance to these promises in this psalm. These are not written for our inspiration but for our protection. These are not words of comfort in affliction but words of *deliverance* from affliction.

11

No Plague Comes Near My Family

No evil will befall you,
Nor will any plague come near your tent.
Psalm 91:10

Are you worried about your family? This part of Psalm 91 is written in capital letters just for you. After God repeats our part of the condition in verse nine, He then reemphasizes the promise in verse ten: "Nor will any plague come near your tent (your household)." It is at this point in the psalm that the Bible makes this covenant more comprehensive than just being about ourselves.

God has just added a new dimension to the promise: the opportunity to exercise faith not only for ourselves, but also for the protection of our entire household. If these promises were only available to us as individuals, they would not be very comforting. Because God has created within us both an instinct to be protected and a need to protect those who belong to us, He has assured us here that these promises are for each of us and our households.

It appears that the Old Testament leaders had a better understanding of this concept than we who are under the New Covenant. That is why Joshua chose for himself and for his household.

> "If it is disagreeable in your sight to serve the LORD, choose for yourselves today whom you will serve…but as for me and my house, we will serve the LORD."
> (Joshua 24:15)

As Joshua made the decision that his household would serve God with him, he was influencing their destiny and declaring their protection at the same time. In much the same way, Rahab bargained with the Israeli spies for her whole family (see Joshua 2:13).

When our hearts are truly steadfast and when we are trusting in His faithfulness to fulfill His promises, we'll not be constantly afraid that something bad is going to happen to one of our family members.

> He will not fear evil tidings; His heart is steadfast, trusting in the LORD. (Psalm 112:7)

Negative expectations will begin to pass away and we will start expecting good reports. According to this verse, we can grab our ears and proclaim, "These ears were made to hear good tidings." The fear of bad tidings can plague our very existence. That fear of the phone ringing in the night, of that knock on the door, or of the siren of an ambulance. This is the verse that promises that a steadfast heart will not live in constant fear of tragic news. Someone once said, "Fear knocked, faith answered, and no one was there." When fear knocks, let your mouth say out loud: "I will not fear evil tidings; my heart is steady, trusting in You!"

Several years ago as I was cooking breakfast, Jack walked into the kitchen with one of the glands under his chin so swollen it looked as though he'd attempted to swallow a softball that had lodged on one side of his throat. I rushed him to a physician friend, and thought I could tell by the expression on the doctor's face that he was concerned. When the first words out of his mouth were, "I am going to call in another doctor to have a look at you," my worst fear was confirmed. I knew he suspected that something was seriously wrong.

Right then, the enemy tried to unload a whole carload of fear thoughts and fear pictures in my mind—but when God's Word has been stored in the heart, it has a way of surfacing just when it's needed. The Scripture in Psalm 91:10, "No evil will befall you, Nor will any plague come near your tent," was more than just a comforting thought. It brought life and hope to the situation.

I sat in the second doctor's waiting room, thanking God for this promise and rejoicing over the outcome long before the doctor ever poked his smiling face around the corner to tell me that everything was fine. It turned out to be just a sore throat that had settled in the gland on one side of Jack's throat. Even the swelling had gone down by the next morning.

It is so rewarding to have Psalm 91 promises that include more than just ourselves. It is a *family* that is under that umbrella of protection, based on the extension of this promise in verse ten that moves us from just the individual to the household.

In Matthew 13:32, Jesus makes reference to a mustard seed starting as an herb but growing into a tree with birds nesting in the branches. Others can find protection in our faith, as well, when we plant the seed of the Word.

Towns are one big collection of families, and family protection could not have been more clearly demonstrated than by what took place in Seadrift, Texas, during World War II. The town's citizens decided to pray Psalm 91 collectively over every one of their husbands, sons, grandsons, cousins, uncles, and friends who were going to war. A bulletin board was made with photos of every serviceman and a commitment made that every single day, intercessors would cover them in prayer. Every time they met they would read from Psalm 91.

It seemed that everyone had a family member who had gone to fight. What a testimony to this promise of family protection when every single man returned safely home from war-from all over the world. This town did not suffer a *single* combat casualty while so many other towns and families experienced much grief and heartache, and often, multiple casualties.

The beauty of this psalm is that when someone prays for more than himself, he brings the entire family under the shield of God's Word. It is an added dimension to us as individuals to be able to apply the richness of this covenant to our entire household. What a joy to know you have promises in Psalm 91 that will not only protect you but also those in your family and near your dwelling.

I thank God for this added dimension of being able to apply His covenant umbrella of protection for our entire household. What a joy it is to know that our family is safe.

12

Angels Watching Over Me

For He will give His angels charge concerning you,
To guard you in all your ways.
They will bear you up in their hands,
That you do not strike your foot against a stone.
Psalm 91:11-12

In verses eleven and twelve, God makes another unique promise concerning an additional dimension of our protection. This is one of the most precious promises of God, and He put it right here in Psalm 91. In fact, this is one of the promises Satan used to test Jesus.

Most Christians read past this promise with very little, if any, thought about the magnitude of what is being said. Only after we get to heaven will we realize all the things from which we were spared because of the intervention of God's angels on our behalf.

I am sure you have read stories about missionaries whose lives were spared because would-be murderers saw large bodyguards protecting them—when in fact, there was no one there in the natural. And we can all recall close calls where we escaped a tragedy and there was no explanation in the natural. It is possible to entertain angels without knowing it, as it says in Hebrews 13:2. Sadly, I believe most Christians have a tendency to disregard the ministry of angels altogether.

Floyd Bowers, a friend of ours who worked in the mines in Clovis, New Mexico, had the responsibility of setting off explosives. One particular day he was ready to push the switch when someone tapped him on the shoulder. To his surprise, no one was anywhere around. Deciding that it must have been his imagination, he prepared once again to detonate the explosion when he felt another tap on his shoulder. Again, no one was there. Floyd decided to move all the ignition equipment several hundred feet back up the tunnel. When he finally plunged the charger, the whole top of the tunnel caved in exactly where he had been standing.

A coincidence? You could never make our friend believe that. He knew someone had tapped him on the shoulder.

Verse eleven of Psalm 91 says, "For He will give His angels charge concerning you." What does that mean? Think with me for a moment. Have you ever taken charge of a situation? When you take charge of something, you put yourself in a place of leadership. You begin telling everyone what to do and how to do it. If angels are taking charge of the things that concern us, God has given the angels, not the circumstances, the authority to act on our behalf. That same truth is repeated in Hebrews.

Are they [angels] not all ministering spirits, sent

out to render service for the sake of those who will inherit salvation? (Hebrews 1:14)

Have you ever been fishing on a lake in the middle of the night? Some people think that is the very best time to catch fish. When my husband was seven years old, all the people who worked for his father took their boats to Lake Brownwood to do some night fishing. Jack was placed in a boat with five adults so he would be well supervised. Since one of the men in the boat was an expert swimmer, his mother and dad thought he would be in especially good hands.

Later that night during one of the times when the boats were going back and forth to shore for bait, Jack had gotten out of his boat and into another one without anyone noticing. Then off they went-without Jack-back onto the lake in the dark. This was back before there were rules about life jackets and lights on your fishing boats, so no one could see in the dark what actually happened. Perhaps they hit a stump. But for some reason, the boat Jack had been in sank. All five of the people in it drowned, even the expert swimmer. It became obvious that Jack had been directed to another boat by angels who serve God and are sent to help those who will receive salvation.

When we look to God as the source of our protection and provision, the angels are constantly rendering us aid and taking charge of our affairs. Psalm 103:20

says, "His angels, mighty in strength…Obeying the voice of His word!" As we proclaim God's Word, the angels hasten to carry it out.

Verse eleven also says that angels will guard you in all your ways. Have you ever seen a soldier standing guard, protecting someone? That soldier stands at attention: alert, watchful, and ready to protect at the first sign of attack. How much more will God's angels stand guard over God's children, alert and ready to protect them at all times? Do we believe that? Have we ever even thought about it? Faith is what releases this promise to work on our behalf. How comforting it is to know that God has placed these heavenly guards to have charge over us.

Psalm 91 names so many different avenues through which God protects us. It is exciting to realize from studying this Old Testament psalm that protection is not just an idea in God's mind-He is committed to it. Angelic protection is just another of the unique ways in which God provides that protection. What an unusual idea to add actual beings designed to protect us. He charged angels to guard us in all our ways.

13

The Enemy Under My Feet

You will tread upon the lion and cobra,
The young lion and the serpent you will trample down.
Psalm 91:13

Here in verse thirteen, God transitions to another topic. He takes us from the subject of our being protected by Him and puts emphasis on the authority in His name that has been given to us as believers.

Make a note of the corresponding New Testament Scripture that deals with the authority that has been given to us:

> "Behold, I [Jesus] have given you authority to tread upon serpents and scorpions, and over all the power of the enemy, and nothing will injure you." (Luke 10:19)

We, as Christians, have been given authority over the enemy. He does not have authority over us! We need to take the time to allow that fact to soak in. However, our authority over the enemy is not automatic.

My husband says that too many Christians take authority when they should be praying, and they pray when they should be taking authority. For the most part, Jesus prayed at night and took authority all day. When we encounter the enemy is not the time to start praying. We need to be already "prayed up." When we encounter the enemy, we need to be speaking forth the authority that we have in the name of Jesus.

If a gunman suddenly faced you, would you be confident enough in your authority that you could boldly declare, "I am in covenant with the living God, and I have a blood covering that protects me from anything that you might attempt to do. So in the name of Jesus, I command you to put down that gun"?

If we do not have that kind of courage, then we need to meditate on the authority Scriptures until we become confident in who we are in Christ. At new birth we immediately have enough power placed at our disposal to tread upon the enemy without being harmed. Most Christians, however, either do not know it or they fail to use it. How often do we believe the Word enough to act on it?

Now let's look at what this verse is actually saying. What good does it do to have authority over lions and cobras unless we are in Africa or India or someplace like that? What does the Word mean when it says we will tread on the lion, the young lion, the cobra, and the serpent (translated as *dragon* in the *Holy Bible,* King James Version)? This is a graphic illustration of things that are potentially harmful in our daily lives. These terms are just an unforgettable means of describing the different types of satanic oppression that come against us. So what do these terms mean to us today? Let's break them down.

First of all, there are "lion problems"—those problems that are bold, loud, and forthright—problems that come out in the open and hit us face on. At one time or another we have all had something come against us that was blatant and overt. It might have been a car wreck or a boss who chewed us out royally in front of our fellow employees. Or it might have been an unexpected bill at the end of the month that caused a chain reaction of checks bouncing. Those are lion problems, obvious difficulties that often seem insurmountable. Yet God says that we will tread on them—they will not tread on us.

The "young lions" can grow into full-grown problems if we don't handle them. These young lion problems come against us to harass and destroy gradually, like little foxes. Subtle negative thoughts that tell us we will not survive or that our mate no longer loves us or that we are no longer in love with our mate are good examples of this category. And those little foxes will grow into big ones if they are not taken captive and destroyed (2 Corinthians 10:4-5). Answer those little foxes with the Word of God. Small harassments, distractions, and irritations are young lions.

"Catch the foxes for us,
The little foxes that are ruining the
vineyards,
While our vineyards are in
blossom." (Song of Solomon 2:15)

Next, God names "cobra" problems. These are
the problems that seem to sneak up on us like a snake
in the grass throughout our day. They are what we
might call an undercover attack that brings sudden
death-a deceptive scheme that keeps us blinded until
it devours us.

How many times have you witnessed an unexpected church split or a marriage that fell apart so
suddenly that you couldn't imagine what had hap-
pened-only to find out later that there had been
offenses, gossip, and undermining of authority going
on behind the scenes? By the time the cause was
uncovered, the poison had had its effect on its victims.
Puncture wounds from fangs are hard to detect, and
no one sees the poison as it travels through a body,
but the results are always damaging, and oftentimes
deadly. We definitely need God's protection from
cobra attacks.

The previous figurative examples we might have
guessed, but what are the "dragon" problems? I
looked up that Hebrew word in the *Strong's
Concordance* and it listed "sea monster." First of all,

there is no such thing as a dragon or a sea monster. Dragons are a figment of one's imagination. But have you ever experienced fears that were a figment of your imagination? Sure you have-we all have!

Dragon problems represent our unfounded fears-phantom or mirage fears. That sounds harmless enough, but are you aware that phantom fears can be as deadly as reality fears if we believe them?

Some people's dragon fears are as real to them as another person's lion problems. That is why it is important to define your fears. So many people spend all of their lives running from something that is not even chasing them.

> The wicked flee when no one is pursuing... (Proverbs 28:1)

This verse is a good definition of phantom fears. We have had a great many people share testimonies of God's deliverance from things like fear of the unknown, fear of the dark, fear of clowns, fear of dolls, fear of vampires, fear of facing the future alone, fear of loss, fear of death, tormenting suspicions, claustrophobia, etc. Television and horror movies have built some very realistic imaginary fears. Fantasy fears can cause us to do a lot of unnecessary running in life, so authority over dragons is not just a mental game.

But the good news is that God says that we will tread on all of the powers of the enemy-no matter how loud and bold, sneaky and deceptive, or imaginary the fears. God has given us authority over all of them!

No longer are we to put up with the paralyzing fears that, at one time, gripped our hearts and left us powerless at the sight of the evil that was striking all around us. God has given us His power of attorney, and these problems now have to submit to the authority of His name.

I like that word *tread*. It places all these categories under our feet. I think of a tank crossing a brushy plain. Where the tank treads go, everything is crushed and left flat on the ground. It is a great picture of our authority over these spiritual enemies as well, treading like a tank and crushing all that is evil in our path. That is a strong description of our authority in walking over the lion, young lion, cobra, and dragon.

14

Because I Love Him

"Because he has loved Me, therefore I will..."
Psalm 91:14a

In verses fourteen through sixteen of Psalm 91, the author changes from talking in third person about God's promises to God speaking to us personally from His secret place and announcing promises in the first person. It is a dramatic shift in tone as it moves to God speaking prophetically to each one of us directly, denoting significantly more depth in the relationship.

In these three verses He gives seven promises with as much obvious triumph as a man has when a woman accepts his proposal. A commitment to love involves choice. When you pick one person out of all others, you set your love on that one and embark on a deeper relationship. That is the picture of how God sets His love on us. Love is the cohesiveness that binds man to God, and God will be faithful to His beloved. Love always requires presence and nearness. Special memories are birthed out of relationship. That is why these verses cannot be fully explained, but must be experienced. Let me give you an illustration.

If you are a parent, you may have watched in horror as your young child picked up a newly birthed kitten by the throat and carried it all over the yard. You may have wondered how it ever survived. It was an old red hen that endured the distress dished out by our very enthusiastic children.

Ole Red would allow herself to be picked up while in the process of laying her egg and would deposit it right in Angie's eager little hands. The children had some merit to what they advertised as the freshest eggs in town—a few times the egg never hit the nest. Nesting season had its own special fascination for the children as they watched Ole Red try to hatch out more eggs than she could sit on. The kids would number the eggs in pencil to ensure that each egg was properly rotated and kept warm. They would wait out the twenty-one days and then, with contagious delight, call me out to see the nest swarming with little ones. That old hen had a brood of chicks that was hatched out of eggs from every hen in the henhouse.

Observing a setting hen this close had its own rare charm, as one could witness the protection she gave those chicks in a way most people never have the chance to observe. I remember her feathers as she fanned them out. I remember the smell of the fresh straw the kids kept in the nest. I remember that I could see through that soft, downy underside and watch the rhythmic beating of her heart. Those chicks had an almost enviable position—something that all the books on the theology of protection could never explain in mere words. This was the unforgettable picture of a real-life understanding of what it means to be under the wings. Those were some happy chicks! True protection has everything to do with closeness.

Some people acknowledge that there is a God; others know Him. Neither maturity nor education nor family heritage nor even a lifetime as a nominal Christian can make a person "know" Him. Only an encounter with the Lord and time spent with Him will cause one to lay hold of the promises in these verses of Psalm 91.

We need to ask ourselves, "Do I really love Him?" Jesus even asked this of Peter, a close disciple (see John 21:15). Can you imagine how Peter must have felt when Jesus asked three times, "Peter, do you love Me?" Even so, we need to question ourselves, because these promises are made only to those who have genuinely set their love on Him. Take special note of the fact that these seven promises are reserved for those who return His love.

And remember that the Lord said in John 14:15, "If you love Me, you will keep My commandments." Our obedience is a reliable, telltale sign that shows we really love Him. Do you love Him? If you do, these promises are for you!

15

God Is My Deliverer

"Because he has loved Me, therefore I will deliver him..."
Psalm 91:14a

A promise of deliverance is the first of the seven promises made to the one who loves God. Make it personal! For instance, I quote it like this: "Because I love You, Lord, I thank You that You have promised to deliver me."

When I was young I personally needed deliverance. I almost destroyed my marriage, my family, and my reputation because I was tormented with fear. One incident opened the door. I can remember the very instant my happy life changed into a nightmare that lasted eight years. And one verse walked me out of this living mental hell: "And it will come about that whoever calls on the name of the LORD will be delivered" (Joel 2:32). Many of you desperately need God's promise of deliverance. The Word worked for me and it will work for you.

There are also other types of deliverances. There is the internal and the external. Ask yourself, "From what is He going to deliver me?" Remember the external deliverances discussed in previous chapters.

God will deliver us from all of the following:

Lion problems

Young lion problems

Cobra problems
Dragon problems
Terror by night (evils that come through man-war terror, violence)
Arrows that fly by day (the enemy assignments sent to wound)
Pestilence (plagues, deadly diseases, fatal epidemics)
Destruction (evils over which man has no control)

In other words, God wants to deliver us from every evil known to mankind. What a promise. I thank God that He is the God of deliverance!

> You are my hiding place; You preserve me from trouble; You surround me with songs of deliverance. (Psalm 32:7)

Deliverance is all encompassing. It happens internally and externally; in fact, it surrounds us.

16

I Am Seated with Christ Jesus

"Because he has loved Me...I will set him securely on high, because he has known My name."
Psalm 91:14

To be set securely on high is the second promise to those who love the Lord and know Him by name. "It is My name," God says, "that has been on his lips when he faces troubles, and he has run to Me. He has called out to Me in faith; therefore, I will set him on high."

> ...which He brought about in Christ, when He raised Him from the dead and seated Him at His right hand in the heavenly *places,* far above all rule and authority and power and dominion, and every name that is named, not only in this age, but also in the one to come...and raised us up with Him, and seated us with Him in the heavenly *places,* in Christ Jesus. (Ephesians 1:20-21; 2:6)

It is interesting that God pulls us up to where He is. Things look better from higher up. Our vantage point is greatly improved seated with Him on high.

Notice that this verse emphasizes the word *known*. These promises come from a "knowing" relationship. There are two types of knowing. Hebrews 8:11 quotes Jeremiah speaking of the New Covenant that was to come and comparing it to the Old Testament, in effect saying, "They will no longer say, 'Know (*Strong's Concordance*: to have knowledge of) the Lord.'" Most people under the Old Testament, according to Jeremiah, only had *knowledge* about God-they just had an acquaintance with Him. However, the writer uses a different word, *know*, in the same verse to describe our knowledge of God under the New Covenant.

The second time the word *know* is used in Hebrews 8:11, according to the *Strong's Concordance*, it means "to stare at, discern clearly, to experience or to gaze with wide open eyes as though gazing at something remarkable." When God refers to our knowing Him today, He is referring to something much more personal than what people experienced during Old Testament times. This promise of being seated securely on high is for the one who experiences God intimately.

Read this verse paraphrased and in first person: "Lord, You have promised that You will set me securely on high because I have known Your name on a first-hand basis. I have experienced Your covenant promises brought forth in your different covenant names."

What does verse fourteen mean when it says that we have known His name? Interestingly, under the old covenant, when God wanted to reveal something more about Himself or when He wanted to reveal another portion of His promise, He would introduce Himself by another one of His covenant names. Throughout the Bible, we find God's covenant names and promises—everything from God revealing Himself as Jehovah Jireh (The Lord is our Provider) to Jehovah Shalom (The Lord is our Peace) to Jehovah Rapha (The Lord is our Healer). However, Psalm 91 contains a special, and powerful, list of names for God.

In the first two sentences of Psalm 91 alone, the psalmist refers to God by four different names, progressively denoting stronger relationship. The writer refers to God as the Most High, revealing that He is the highest thing that exists. This implies much more significance when we realize we are set securely on high with the One who is Most High. From on high we have a better vantage point and better perspective. In this opening of Psalm 91, God is also called the Almighty, denoting that He is "all" mighty-the most powerful. Next he is referred to as the Lord, revealing ownership. Then he calls Him My God, making it personal. We see God unveiled in four unique ways to the man who has known His name.

17

God Answers My Call

"He will call on Me, and I will answer him…"
Psalm 91:15a

God makes a third promise here in verse fifteen that He will answer those who truly love Him and call on His name (in His will). Are we aware of what a wonderful promise God is making to us here?

> This is the confidence which we have before Him, that, if we ask anything according to His will, He hears us. And if we know that He hears us in whatever we ask, we know that we have the requests which we have asked from Him.
> (1 John 5:14-15)

Nothing gives me more comfort than to realize that every time I pray in line with God's Word, He hears me. And if He hears me, I know I have the request for which I asked. This one promise keeps me continually searching His Word in order to understand His will and His promises, so that I can know how to pray more effectively.

Sometimes I just ask God for help. When our children were teenagers, we gave them our Chevrolet Classic Impala. To our utter surprise, we all came home one day to find it missing from the carport. The sheriff's department did all the necessary investigation, then told us it was foolish to ever expect to see the car again-that by this time we could be almost certain that it was across the Mexican border with a brand new paint job.

With two teenagers, we needed that second car, so we started calling on God. It took a little effort to do what we knew we must-to forgive our assailant and pray for him. I can't say that there was much more than a grain of mustard seed faith, but with all we could muster, we continued to call on God.

One week to the day after the car was discovered missing from the carport, a young man turned himself in to the police, saying that he had stolen things all of his life but this was the first time he had ever felt guilty. He confessed to stealing our car and told them where he had left it. Sure enough, there it was, exactly where he had said, on the parking lot of the rodeo grounds in a small town not far from Brownwood.

Sometimes we're guilty of just letting the car go and accepting what people say instead of calling on God and believing Him to answer. But God's Word tells us that "whoever believes [trusts] in Him will not be disappointed" (Romans 10:11).

I remember the young man who saved my grandson from drowning in a swimming pool. When James realized he couldn't get Cullen off the bottom of the pool because of Cullen's size, he did what this verse recommends. Instead of panicking and giving up, James called on God. (James tells this story in his own words in the *Psalm 91* youth edition.) We need to teach our children to call on God at a young age. Sometimes, however, our children can teach us a thing or two, as you can see in this next story about our son.

Jack and our son, Bill, not knowing there was an old underground gas well at the back of our three-hundred-acre property, were burning brush. As you can imagine, when the fire got over the well it literally exploded, sending fire in every direction and igniting a tall, dry field of grass nearby. Immediately the fire was completely out of control. With no water lines back there, they were fighting to no avail. The barrel of water they had in the back of the pickup didn't even make a dent in the flames.

Seeing that the fire was getting dangerously close to other fields that fed right in to the surrounding homes, Jack flew up to the house to call the fire department, sent me to meet them at the crossroads so they wouldn't get lost, and then dashed back—only to find that the fire was out. Bill, looking like he'd been working in the coal mines, was sitting on a tree stump trying to catch his breath.

Jack said, "How on earth were you able to put out the fire? There was no way." Bill's next words—"I called on God"—said it all.

You, too, can be delivered from destruction. For those out-of-control days, God is always there.

18

God Rescues Me from Trouble

"...I will be with him in trouble; I will rescue him..."
Psalm 91:15

The fourth promise—to *rescue from trouble* those who love the Lord—is found in the middle of verse fifteen. It is a well-known fact that human nature cries out to God when faced with trouble. Men in prison, soldiers in war, people in accidents—all seem to call out to God when they get in a crisis. Even atheists are known to call on the God they don't acknowledge when they are extremely afraid.

A lot of criticism has been given to those kinds of court-of-the-last-resort prayers. However, in defense of this kind of praying, we must remember that when one is in pain, he usually runs to the one he loves the most and the one he trusts. The alternative is not calling out at all, so this verse acknowledges that calling out to God in trouble is a good place for a person to start.

If a person has never felt danger, he never thinks about needing protection. It is the one that knows he is in imminent danger who will appreciate and take the words of this psalm to heart. God has a great deal of variety in His plentiful means of protection and modes of rescue from trouble.

This verse also reminds me of a story I read about

a U.S. senator living in pre-Civil War days, a story that is said to be true. The senator had taken his son to the slave market, where the boy noticed a black mother crying and praying as traders were preparing to sell her daughter on the slave block. As he walked closer, he overheard the mother crying out, "Oh, God, if I could help You as easily as You could help me, I'd do it for You, Lord." The young man was so touched by the prayer that he went over and bought the girl off the slave block and gave her back to her mother.

God answers our prayers and rescues us in so many different ways. I am so thankful that He is creative and not limited by our seemingly impossible situations. But we have to ask in faith and not confine Him to our limited resources. God says, "If you love Me, I will be with you when you find yourself in trouble, and I will rescue you." But we have to trust Him to do it His way.

> "When you pass through the waters, I will be with you;
> And through the rivers, they will not overflow you.
> When you walk through the fire, you will not be scorched,
> Nor will the flame burn you."
> (Isaiah 43:2)

I read a story several years ago about a woman who had a son in a war zone in World War II, and she wrote out Psalm 91 and sent it to him, explaining that God's promises in Psalm 91 would be his protection. The son took it to his commanding officer, who assigned his whole outfit to read the entire psalm out loud together every morning. She said that when the war was over, this was one of the few outfits in the war zone that reportedly had not one casualty.

Our son, Bill, once saw the rescuing power of God when he found himself in serious trouble after attempting to swim across a lake that was much wider than he calculated. With no strength left in his body and having already gone under twice, Bill experienced all the sensations of drowning. But miraculously, God not only provided a woman on the opposite bank, which had been deserted, but also enabled her to throw a life ring (that just happened to be near) over thirty yards, landing within inches of his almost lifeless body. That was certainly Bill's day of trouble, but I thank God that He was with Bill and rescued him.

Although some people might call happenings like these a coincidence, the negative situations that we encounter can become God-incidences when we trust His Word.

19

God Honors Me

"I will...honor him."
Psalm 91:15

The fifth promise—to *honor* those who love God—is in the last part of verse fifteen.

All of us like to be honored. I can remember the teacher calling my name when I was in grade school and complimenting my work on a paper I'd turned in. That thrilled me. I was honored.

Several years ago our daughter, Angelia, attended a political rally in our city that was given for George W. Bush when he was campaigning for governor of Texas. She had shared a quick anecdote with him at the beginning of the meeting when they first met. After he had spoken to the group and was leaving with some of his colleagues, everyone was shocked when he left his group and darted back to our daughter to say, "Remember the promise I made—no tears for you in November." It honored her that he not only remembered her, but also recalled their conversation.

Our granddaughter's husband, Heath Adams, is a staff sergeant in the U.S. Air Force. He recently finished Airman Leadership School and is stationed at Great Falls, Montana. We were all thrilled when he received the John Levitow Award, the highest award given at the leadership school banquet. It was not only an honor for him, but it was also an honor for his whole squadron. Then he was one of eight people chosen from 4,500 security forces to represent Air Force Space Command in the Defender Challenge Competition, where his team took silver medals in the obstacle course and tactics events, placing second overall.

Heath was also a distinguished graduate at the Security Force Level II Combat Leaders Course. He won the 341st Security Forces Group Noncommissioned Officer of the Year award and the 20th Air Force Noncommissioned Officer of the Year award. Heath also had the honor of giving an integrated tactics initiative brief to the secretary of the Air Force-the first such brief the secretary had ever heard.

Heath's commander coordinated a surprise ceremony to give Heath his promotion and secretly arranged for our granddaughter, Jolena, to be there. Not only was his military service noted, but his character as a family man, a youth pastor, and, ultimately, a faithful follower of Christ–evidenced in his activity with a local church–was communicated to the group. The ceremony honored Heath before all his peers.

Men have many types of customs to honor other men, from ceremonies and speeches to medals of distinction. I have had the highest admiration for each serviceman I've interviewed as they showed me their Purple Hearts and their Medals of Honor. Those are symbols of the honors that have been bestowed on those recipients.

Each year we honor the man who is chosen outstanding man of the year in our city. Civic organizations give plaques every year to honor men and women who have made exceptional contributions. It's an honor and it feels good to have someone we consider important pay special attention to us. It is a thrill to be honored by man—but how much *more* of a tribute and a thrill it is when we are honored by God. Fulfilling our part of the covenant enables God to honor us.

Have you ever thought about what it means to be honored by the God of the universe? He honors us by calling us His sons and daughters. He honors us by answering when we take His Word seriously and call out to Him in faith. He honors us by recognizing us individually and by preparing a place for us to be with Him eternally. Giving us honor is one of the seven unique promises made in Psalm 91.

20

God Satisfies Me with Long Life

"With a long life I will satisfy him."
Psalm 91:16a

The sixth promise of the final verses of Psalm 91 is found in verse sixteen. God does not just say that He will prolong our lives and give us a lot of birthdays. No! He says that He will *satisfy* us with a *long life.* There are people who would testify that just having a great many birthdays is not necessarily a blessing. But God says that He will give us many birthdays, and as those birthdays roll around we will experience satisfaction.

It has been said that there is a God-shaped vacuum inside each of us. Man has tried to fill that vacuum with many different things, but nothing will satisfy that emptiness until it is filled with Jesus. That is the true satisfaction to which God refers in His promise. God is making the offer. If we will come to Him, let Him fill that empty place on the inside, and allow Him to fulfill the call on our lives, then He will give us a long life and satisfy us as we live it out. Only the dissatisfied person can really appreciate what it means to find satisfaction.

It is a fact that God wants us to live a satisfied life, but let's not neglect the promise of a long life. King David was Israel's most valiant, daring warrior, yet he lived to be a ripe old age—"full of days," as the Old Testament authors liked to say. His life was filled with combat, high-risk situations, and impossible odds. Yet he did not die in battle; his head went down in peace in his old age. Long life is a great concluding promise of protection.

Paul lets us know in Ephesians, however, that we are in a fight. We can't flow with the wide road, with what feels good, and still win this battle, because the enemy will make the wrong path extremely easy to take. Eddie Rickenbacker, the World War I flying ace who had near-death experiences throughout his life, once wanted to let himself die, but later said this about death: "I felt the presence of death, and I knew that I was going. You may have heard that dying is unpleasant, but don't you believe it. Dying is the sweetest, tenderest, most sensuous sensation I have ever experienced. Death comes disguised as a sympathetic friend. All was serene; all was calm. How wonderful it would be simply to float out of this world. It is easy to die. You have to fight to live. And that is what I did. I recognized that wonderful, mellow sensation for what it was—death—and I fought it. I literally fought death in my mind, pushing away the sweet blandishments and welcoming back the pain. The next ten days were a continuous fight with the old Grim Reaper, and again and again, I would feel myself start to slip away. Each time I rallied and fought back, until I had turned the corner toward recovery."

Captain Rickenbacker should know! Death came toward him many times-during his service as a soldier in both world wars, when he survived two plane crashes, and when he was lost for twenty-four days on the Pacific Ocean.

Sometimes the spirit of death makes a bid for our very life. It is these inner dynamics that are at work when a person is wounded, facing a serious illness, wracked by pain from an injury, or sensing impending doom. It is easy to give in to it. We think of the ugly side to destruction, but the danger is when it comes with a pretty face. It is a *fight* to break free from the enticing call of death, persevere to victory, and receive the covenant promise of a satisfied, long life.

Once, in a boat on the Sea of Galilee, the disciples cried out in fear that they would drown in a storm. Jesus, however, had said that they must go to the other side. If they had thought through what He'd said, they would have known the storm would not harm them because they had His word on a mission across the lake. In the same way, if you have been promised a satisfied, long life, then you know you will make it through the present circumstances.

God wants us to claim the promise of long life, but He also wants us to live that long life for Him. Ask yourself: "What *am* I going to do with my long life?"

21

I Behold His Salvation

"...and let him behold My salvation."
Psalm 91:16b

Allowing those who love Him to behold His salvation is the seventh promise found in the last part of verse sixteen. God wants us to take hold of His salvation.

The movement of this last line in Psalm 91 describes our ultimate, final victory. The order of this sentence gives us the promise that we will see salvation face to face, *during* and *after* our long, satisfied life. This moves us beyond an intellectual knowledge of salvation to relationship. It secures our future, but it starts now. Jesus constantly reminded us that, "Salvation is now! Today it has come!" Many people are surprised when they look up the word "salvation" in a Bible concordance and find that it has a much deeper meaning than just a ticket to heaven. We often miss the richness of this promise.

According to *Strong's Exhaustive Concordance,* the word *salvation* includes health, healing, deliverance, rescue, safety, protection, and provision. What more could we ask? God promises that He will allow us to see and take hold of His health, His healing, His deliverance, His protection, and His provision!

Many people read Psalm 91 and simply see it with their eyes, but very few behold it in their lives.

My prayer is for that to change. One of my biggest thrills is when people write or call after I've taught this truth and they describe the ecstatic joy of having it come alive in their heart. I love to hear the extent to which they have actually taken hold of this covenant and started experiencing it as a vital part of their existence.

In the testimonies that follow, your heart will be encouraged by those who have beheld firsthand the salvation of the Lord. Read their stories in their own words. The truth about God's salvation-His protection, deliverance, health, and provision-is more than just wishful thinking. It is a promise of which one can actually take hold.

Summary

Nothing in this world is more reliable than God's promises when we believe them, refuse to waver, and decide to make His Word our final authority for every area of life.

I believe that Psalm 91 is a covenant—a spiritual contract—that God has made available to His children. It is desperately needed in these difficult days. There are some who sincerely ask, "How do you know that you can take a song from the psalms and base your life on it?" Jesus answered that question. The value of the psalms was emphasized when He cited them as a source of Truth that must be fulfilled.

> Now He said to them, "These are My words which I spoke to you while I was still with you, that all things which are written about Me in the Law of Moses and the Prophets *and the Psalms* must be fulfilled [emphasis added]."
> (Luke 24:44)

When Jesus specifically equates the psalms to the law of Moses and the prophets, we see that the psalms are historically relevant, prophetically sound, and totally applicable and reliable.

At a time when there are so many uncertainties facing us, it is more than comforting to know that God not only knows ahead of time what we will be facing, but He also makes absolute provision for us.

Someone once pointed out, "It is interesting that the world must have gotten its distress 911 number from God's answer to our distress call–Psalm 91-1."

It seems only a dream now to think back on the time when my mind was reeling in fears and doubts. Little did I know when I asked God that pertinent question-"Is there any way for a Christian to escape all the evils that are coming on this world?"–He was going to give me a dream that would not only change my life, but also change the lives of thousands of others who would hear and believe.

Our minds cannot even begin to comprehend God's goodness. TRULY, WHAT A MIGHTY GOD WE SERVE.

What Must I Do To Be Saved?

We've talked about physical protection. Now let's make sure that you have eternal protection. The promises from God in this book are for God's children who love Him. If you have never given your life to Jesus and accepted Him as your Lord and Savior, there is no better time than right now.

> "There is none righteous, not even one." (Romans 3:10)

> For all have sinned and fall short of the glory of God. (Romans 3:23)

God loves you and gave His life that you might live eternally with Him.

> But God demonstrates His own love toward us, in that while we were yet sinners, Christ died for us. (Romans 5:8)

> For God so loved the world [you], that He gave His only begotten Son, that whoever believes in Him shall not perish, but have eternal life. (John 3:16)

There is nothing we can do to earn our salvation or to make ourselves good enough to go to heaven. It is a free gift!

> For the wages of sin is death,
> but the free gift of God is eternal
> life in Christ Jesus. (Romans 6:23)

There is also no other avenue through which we can reach heaven other than Jesus Christ-God's Son.

> "And there is salvation in no
> one else; for there is no other name
> under heaven that has been given
> among men, by which we must be
> saved." (Acts 4:12)

> Jesus said to him, "I am the way,
> and the truth, and the life; no one
> comes to the Father but through
> Me." (John 14:6)

You must believe that Jesus is the Son of God, that He died on the cross for your sins, and that He rose again on the third day.

> ...who [Jesus] was declared the Son
> of God with power by the resurrec-
> tion from the dead... (Romans 1:4)

You may be thinking, *How do I accept Jesus and become His child?* God in His love has made it so easy.

> If you confess with your mouth Jesus as Lord, and believe in your heart that God raised Him from the dead, you will be saved.
> (Romans 10:9)

> But as many as received Him, to them He gave the right to become children of God, even to those who believe in His name. (John 1:12)

It is as simple as praying a prayer similar to this one—if you sincerely mean it in your heart:

> Dear God:
> I believe You gave your Son, Jesus, to die for me. I believe He shed His blood to pay for my sins and that You raised Him from the dead so I can be Your child and live with You eternally in heaven. I am asking Jesus to come into my heart right now and save me. I confess Him as the Lord and Master of my life.
> I thank You, dear Lord, for loving

me enough to lay down Your life
for me. Take my life now and use it
for Your glory. I ask for all that You
have for me.
In Jesus' name,
Amen

Psalm 91 Testimonies

Jennifer McCullough

Jennifer McCullough is a twenty-five-year-old Howard Payne University graduate serving as a preteen minister in Dallas, Texas, while working on her master of education degree at Southwestern Baptist Theological Seminary.

Before leaving for East Africa in 1999, I was being discipled by Angelia Schum, my college Bible study teacher. It was a crash course in everything you need to know before entering "the bush!" I ran into her friend Donna Crow one night at church. She said, "You do know about Psalm 91, don't you?" When I said, "No," she said, "Angie must not love you very much if she hasn't told you about Psalm 91!"

I began intently studying the psalm and memorized it before I left. I had no idea of the power of this passage until January 15, 2000. I lived in a village in the bush with the Ankole tribe (cattle herders), working with orphans with AIDS and teaching at the village school. I often found myself praying Psalm 91 while walking the circumference of the village. I had gone to the city the day before on the milk truck. That night, I was lying in my hut and heard gunshots. I ran to a fellow missionary's hut and sat in a small room praying Psalm 91 over and over. The husband was out investigating, so it was just a twenty-four-year-old mother, her two-year-old child, and me.

A group of rebels was raiding my village. Men were shot, a pregnant woman was beaten, villagers were robbed, and cattle were stolen. The villagers were laid out in a line on their stomachs with guns and machetes pointed to their heads; they were told not to say a word. The raid was well planned, as they had been watching us for days from the bushes.

Here is the miracle! Village people know that white missionaries have more in their huts than Ugandans make in a lifetime. Yet the rebels never came to our hut-in spite of the fact that everyone else's hut was raided. After the fact, the rebels admitted to the police that they had followed the milk truck through the bush the night before the raid. I had been on that truck sitting next to the driver who was carrying two million shillings—the villagers' monthly income from the milk sales. They did not attack the truck en route because we had returned before dark that night. This was the first time we had ever returned before dark in the six months I had been riding the route.

The day after the attack was very intense. I walked through the village, praying for villagers who had been robbed and beaten. They had looks of pure terror on their faces, knowing that the rebels were still hiding in the bush nearby. While talking to the villagers, no one could believe that I was not attacked. My interpreter, Segambe, said, "It was as if your hut was not even there."

God is faithful! He has a perfect plan for your life! God is all knowing! He will give you weapons to fight the battles you face.

God did not give Psalm 91 only to missionaries in the African bush. He gave it to everyone so that we can daily claim His promises to us as Christians. I find the words of Psalm 91 in my daily prayers: "...He will cover you with His feathers, and under His wings you may find refuge. His faithfulness will be your shield and rampart..."

Don't miss the chance to see the power of God's promises in your life. Claim them, memorize them, pray them, and live them. He is faithful!

Julie's Miracle as told by her father, Dr. James Crow

Julie's miracle is told by her father, Dr. James Crow, a dentist in Brownwood, Texas.

Julie's ordeal began in May 1983 while she attended a friend's birthday party in the country. Julie had ridden horses with her grandfather for nearly nine of her ten years, so when they asked who wanted to ride she jumped at the chance. But a ten-year-old riding bareback on a grown horse has very little to hold onto-so when the horse began to run she slipped under its belly. And between the rocks and the hooves she received a very serious head injury.

When we arrived at the hospital a physician friend tried to be a buffer for us before we saw our daughter. He warned us that she was in very serious condition and that the hospital was already making arrangements to have her transported to the nearest large city for treatment. Even with his attempt to prepare us, we were still not anywhere close to being prepared for what we saw. The right side of her head was swollen literally to the size of a volleyball, both eyes were swollen shut, and her hair and face were drenched in blood. There was no way we could have recognized her.

I need, at this point, to interject some crucial information. Through the teachings of Kenneth Copeland of Copeland Ministries in Fort Worth, I had started doing a great deal of study on healing and faith. Jesus and I had spent a lot of time alone together, during which I had received the baptism of the Holy Spirit and the Lord had become very personal to me. And our church was strong on believing that Jesus is still the "Healer." I can truly say that from the instant I first saw Julie's condition, I called on Jesus and totally expected that His healing power and His promises in Psalm 91 would bring her through. I'm glad I didn't have to analyze the situation, but we all knew it was so bad that we had to have a miracle. Even before the ambulance reached the hospital, there was a growing network of believers who were interceding.

In addition to the driver, there were two paramedics in the back of the ambulance with Julie and one in the front between the driver and me. I prayed all the way-just in a whisper-almost oblivious to the others in the cab. I remember thanking Jesus for her healing and telling Satan that he couldn't have Julie-that she was a child of God and had been dedicated to the Lord from birth. For the entire eighty-five miles I never stopped claiming her healing. I didn't get loud! I knew I was being heard in both realms of the spirit.

Then, somewhere just short of the city, the paramedics slid open the panel between the back and the cab area and said something to the driver. We had been going fairly fast all the way, but at this point the driver put on his siren and sped the rest of the way to the hospital. I found out later that the paramedics had informed the driver that Julie had lost all vital signs and could not be revived. I'm not sure how long she had no vital signs, but it was more than minutes. I learned that life came back into her body about the time we came to the edge of town.

While all this was happening, my brother-in-law, who was an elder in our church, was about forty-five minutes behind us in his car. On the way he felt that God told him that Julie had died, and God asked him if he would be willing to lay across her body like the prophet Elisha had done with the little boy in 2 Kings 4:34 to bring him back to life. Realizing this meant he would most likely have to push his way past the doctors and nurses and look very foolish, he said that he wrestled with himself for several minutes before knowing without a doubt that he was willing to do it. The moment the commitment was made, he felt God told him Julie would be all right. We later backtracked to the place where he was en route during this confrontation with God. According to our calculations, the ambulance would have been coming into the city limits just about the time God told him that Julie would be all right. That was when her vital signs had returned.

Upon our arrival Julie was immediately taken in for a CAT scan. When the doctor got the results, he gave us no hope whatsoever. Someone asked him if there would be brain damage, and he replied, "Parents always want to ask about brain damage. Your concern needs to be whether or not she will live through the night—but if she does live, yes, there will be extensive brain damage."

I was not arrogant, but I denied each negative statement from anyone who was not standing in faith with us. The doctor was obviously perturbed with us, but I'm sure he just thought we were in denial. He just didn't realize where our denial was coming from. To the doctor's total surprise, Julie did live through the night. We kept healing Scriptures on her pillow at all times and held her and spoke love to her continuously. My wife had the astronomical job of cleaning the dried blood from her hair and untangling it—speaking healing and quoting Psalm 91 over her the whole time.

We were informed we were in for a long stay, but my frustration was that Julie wasn't climbing out of the bed the next day, ready to go home. God must have given me a gift of faith because I was ready for a Lazarus healing. We began to notice that, miraculously, nearly every timetable we were given was accomplished seven times faster. At first we thought it was a neat coincidence, until it continued way beyond any possibility of happenchance.

During the hospital stay of only nine days, we saw our miracle unveil. The physical damage continued to heal at this supernatural rate as the swelling went down, color returned to normal, and mental behavior went from the bizarre to normal—every day was a miracle. There were other patients in the hospital with head injuries, seemingly not nearly as serious as Julie's, who had been there six months and more. Many of them were just learning how to walk and talk again.

During the next few days, we saw Julie protected by Jesus while He was accomplishing her healing. It was as if her body was left on the hospital bed to go through the healing while Julie herself—her soul maybe, for sure her spirit—seemed to retreat inside to be cuddled by Jesus until the healing process was complete. For the first several days after the accident we could not recognize anything about her that reminded us of our Julie. Then, a little at a time, we saw her return until she was totally back to normal. We could almost see the healing taking place before our very eyes. The nurses were amazed. They all called her their "miracle girl."

Even our hardcore neurosurgeon—without giving credit to God—said that her recovery couldn't be explained. He saw us praying and standing and believing day after day, and because of the results before his very eyes, he could not very easily have gone home and called us a bunch of kooks.

On the night of the accident we had been told that in addition to the brain damage, there would be considerable loss of hearing since the mastoid bone had been part of the skull fracture. They were also quite sure that the optic nerve had been damaged, which we were told would cause either total, or at least partial, loss of eyesight.

When Julie was dismissed only nine days after entering the hospital, the only outward sign of the accident was some bloodshot in her right eye. She went home with no brain damage and no loss of eyesight (twenty-twenty vision). On the day of her release, however, the attending physician-even after watching her miraculous recovery—still insisted, "There will be a hearing loss," and he instructed us to take her to the audiologist in July. We did that, only to be told that she had perfect hearing.

We thank Jesus for what He did on the cross for each one of us and for His wonderful promises in Psalm 91.

Julie and her husband, Rocky, live in San Antonio, Texas, where she works as a dental hygienist.

Skylar Chasteen

Audra Chasteen of Brownwood, Texas, gave this testimony following a spectacular demonstration in the life of her son, Skylar, of God's faithfulness to fulfill His promises in Psalm 91.

About 7:30 in the evening on July 28, 2001, three of my sisters and I, along with our children, were visiting my parents. Skylar, my four-year-old, was riding bicycles with the older boys out in the pasture about a half-mile from the house. I had just turned to warn my older son not to ride down the hill because of the steep incline when I realized that Skylar had already started down. The next thing I knew, the bicycle was out of control and he had gone over the side of a cliff.

When I got to Skylar, he wasn't moving and he wasn't crying. He was tangled in the wheel of the bicycle, lying on his stomach with his chin twisted past his shoulder, resting on his shoulder blade. It was a terrifying sight to see Skylar's head bent almost backwards. His left arm was back behind him with his wrist above his right shoulder. His eyes were half open, in a fixed position down and to the corner. He was blue and not breathing.

When I saw Skylar in that distorted position and not breathing, I didn't have to be told that it was bad. I just started screaming. In spite of the obvious head and neck injury, I turned his head forward so that he could breathe. But when he still didn't start breathing, I turned his whole body straight, hoping that would help. When that didn't work, I became hysterical. My three sisters and I are nurses, one RN and three LVN, but we couldn't seem to pull ourselves together to know what to do medically. It was as though none of us had one brain cell functioning. My sister Donna just picked him up and stood there.

When my oldest sister, Cynthia, finally got to the scene of the accident, the first thing she did was to lay her hand over on Skylar's head and start rebuking the enemy. She kept saying, "I rebuke you, Satan, in the name of Jesus-you get your hands off Skylar-you cannot have him!" Then she started pleading the blood of Jesus and quoting Psalm 91 over him. Hearing God's Word coming out of Cynthia's mouth pulled me back to my senses. I sent one of my sisters for her car, and we headed for the nearest hospital-seventeen miles away.

On the way to the hospital we did some rescue breaths on Skylar, and he would breathe for a few minutes and then stop. I tried to hold his head and neck straight, but the whole time his eyes were still fixed. Cynthia and I continued to speak Psalm 91 over Skylar and to command his body to line up with God's Word, but nothing was coming out as eloquently as I wanted. All that I could say was, "Bones, be like you're supposed to be-body, be like you are supposed to be-in Jesus' name."

I remember thinking, *God, how can you ask us to praise You in every situation–how can I praise You when my child is in danger?* And I felt like the Lord impressed on me, "Just do it-you don't have to know why–just do it!" I was able to give God one sentence: "Lord, I give You the glory and the honor and the praise." I wasn't giving God the praise from thinking that He sent this situation; I was giving God the praise because of who He is and because His Word said to praise Him in all things. The whole way we prayed in the Spirit and quoted Psalm 91 over Skylar.

When we got to the hospital in Comanche, Texas, they immediately put a neck brace on Skylar, but he still wasn't responding. By then he had started breathing on his own, but his eyes were still fixed. Then he started throwing up–another sign of a bad head injury.

As soon as they had Skylar in X-ray, I called one of our pastors to get some of the intercessors praying.

I knew we needed help. As much as we had been taught, I was still unprepared when the tragedy actually happened. As he prayed, peace came over me and I suddenly knew that everything was going to be okay.

The X-rays showed an obvious break in the C-1 vertebra (the first vertebra under the head) and Skylar still wasn't responding. He was immediately, with the X-rays, air-flighted to Cook's Children's Hospital in Fort Worth.

Since I was still in my scrubs from working all day, they didn't realize at Cook's Hospital that I was the mother, so they had me helping to draw the blood on Skylar. I was listening as the trauma nurse reported to the doctor when he came in, "He has a C-1 fracture, his eyes are deviated and down to the left, he stopped breathing." The doctor was shocked when he discovered I was the mother. I could never have been that peaceful without all the prayers.

The only thing that seemed to calm Skylar while we were waiting was to put my hand on his forehead and pray Psalm 91 over him. Even though Skylar was not awake through all of this, once when I paused in my praying, Skylar said, "Amen!" From the moment that he responded from an unconscious state, giving his agreement to that prayer, I knew he would be fine, in spite of the seriousness of his condition. Finally they wheeled him in for more X-rays and for a CAT scan to see if there was any bleeding in the brain cavity.

When the doctor finally came in, he had a very strange look on his face, and all he could say was, "He's going to be all right!" Then, after consulting with the radiologist, they came in saying, "We don't know how to explain this, but we can find no head trauma (brain swelling or bleeding) and we cannot find a C-1 fracture." They had the Comanche hospital X-rays with the obvious break, but their X-rays showed no sign of a break.

There are no words to describe the joy and the gratitude and the excitement that we felt at that moment. All the nurses were pouring in to tell us how lucky we were and all I could say was, "Luck had nothing to do with this. This was God!" I was not about to let Satan have one ounce of glory. I knew that it was a miracle and that it was God who had healed Skylar; however, he still wasn't responding very well, so they put us in the pediatric ward of the ICU to monitor him. The next morning the nurse came in and scratched him on the head, assuming she would get the same response (nothing) she had gotten the day before. But this time, when she scratched Skylar and called out his name, he said, "What?" Everyone, including the nurse, jumped-and then rejoiced!

From that point on Skylar was able to wake up and respond. The doctor was just amazed. He said, "I don't know what to tell you. There was definitely a break on that other X-ray, but he is obviously okay now. I don't know how to explain it." He didn't have to explain it. I knew what had happened. God is so good!

Skylar has always been very close to my mother, and I found out something very interesting after we got home. Two weeks prior to the accident, Sklar had been telling her that it was time for him to go be with Jesus. And Mother would say, "No, Skylar, why would you say that? It's not time for you to go be with Jesus." But he would emphatically say, "Yes, it is! I've got to go." And she would argue with him, but she said she didn't think too much about it since he's only four years old. But after the accident my mother knew that there was warfare going on, and it was God's promise in Psalm 91 that finally won the battle.

Since the day we left the hospital, Skylar has been a perfectly normal, healthy little boy with no problems and no side effects from the accident. He is truly a miracle!

Rene Hood

Rene Hood of Bangs, Texas, is the founder of the Root of Jesse prison ministry.

My testimony begins in July 1998. At this point in my life I had eaten almost nothing for approximately two months, yet I continued to gain weight. I could not go outside in the direct sunlight for any length of time without my face becoming irritated to the point that if you placed your hand on my face, the print of your hand would remain there. I had also begun to develop black spots on my face, arms, and legs. Later a red rash appeared on my face and throughout my body. Bruises would appear without my falling or having been hit.

During the month of July, my energy level was so low that it was a challenge to just clean the bathtub after bathing. My body became racked with pain even when I tried performing a task as simple as brushing my teeth. One particular night is still fresh in my memory. For the previous week or so, I had been choking when I'd lie down at night. This night was the same, but when I got up that morning I made the shocking discovery that I couldn't perform normal bodily functions. Knowing that something had to be done quickly, I called my doctor early that morning. After his examination he referred me to Scott and White Hospital to see Dr. Nichols, a nephrologist.

The night prior to my seeing Dr. Nichols, my body aches had reached a new level; it become a norm for me to have a fever of 103 degrees or more. I felt like my brain was frying. I would lie on my bathroom floor in misery. My brown body transformed before my eyes into a gray color, covered with perspiration and rolled up in a fetal position. I told the Lord that it would be so easy to give up the ghost and just go home to be with Him, but I said, "Lord, I know that You are not finished with me. Lord, I hurt so badly, and yet I know that there are people out there that You have called me to touch. My kids need me! I know I am walking in the valley of the shadow of death, but I will fear no evil. You promised me, Lord, in Psalm 91 that only with my eyes would I see the reward of the wicked-that a thousand would fall at my side and ten thousand at my right hand, but it would not come nigh me."

My eighteen-year-old daughter was home for the summer and she took me to see the nephrologist at

Temple Hospital. I was so weak that I could barely walk. After a twenty-five-minute examination, the nephrologist, with no bedside manner and no sense of caring, said, "I give you three months and you will just go 'poop.'" I was very angry that he would speak such words to me in the presence of my daughter, without any sensitivity. Then he said, "It will not be easy because you will be in a lot of pain, but (as he pointed to my daughter) she's big enough–she can take care of herself." Then he walked out the door. I looked at my daughter and assured her, "Mom is not going anywhere."

I was hospitalized, running a high fever and unable to eat. I would have involuntary shakes that I couldn't control and my right lung had collapsed because of the mass of protein my kidneys were now throwing into my system. I looked like a seven-month pregnant woman. My kidneys were shutting down, my joints ached and were swollen, and the doctors had found a mass on my liver. After twelve days of their making one mistake after another and causing me more suffering without my getting any better, I asked my daughter to help me dress and take me back home to Bangs because God was going to give me a miracle.

I am a living testimony of His faithfulness to His promises. I went to my parents' house, where I would sit up and walk as well as I could, reminding God of what He had promised: "You will not be afraid of the deadly pestilence. It will not approach you."

My local doctor would call and remind me that those specialists said I was dying and that I needed to be in a hospital. I wouldn't! I couldn't! I knew that "greater was He that was in me than he that was in the world." I had a supernatural peace that I was well and that the healing would manifest itself soon—so I kept pressing.

Since I would not go back to the hospital and my condition, by sight, was no better, my doctor encouraged me to go to a nephrologist in Abilene, Texas. I finally agreed but refused the medicine because of the side effects. Not one doctor gave me one ounce of hope, but I was determined to receive the healing that Christ had provided.

Then the miracle started manifesting.

It was during those next few months that I gradually started feeling better and my strength started returning. Finally, after seeing the Abilene doctor for two months and once again being put through a battery of tests, he stated, "I'm looking at your paperwork and I'm looking at you. If you had let us do what we wanted to do-and you wouldn't-we doctors would be patting ourselves on the back, saying we had gotten you in remission. All I can say is-whatever you have been doing, just keep doing it." Then he told me that I was a "miracle."

My doctor had a liver specialist meet me at the

Brownwood hospital and after a CAT scan and two sonograms, he could not find any mass in my liver. I was then sent to a blood specialist, and after reading the reports he repeated twice that I was "a wonder." I have seen three Christmases since being told that I would not live to see another Christmas.

My prison ministry didn't suffer and souls continue to be saved, delivered, and set free because I abided in God's Word and trusted Him to be faithful. I expect to have a book out soon called *Being Found in His Word.* We all need to be in His Word, refusing, no matter what, to be driven from His promises. I know that this battle and subsequent victory give honor to a "faithful, loving, and caring God" who desires to be embraced by each one of us.

Dane Kaley

Told by Peggy Joyce Ruth.

Our good friends, Vicki and Gerald Jackson, live in Fort Worth, Texas. One of their fellow church members, Dane Kaley, developed a small growth in his ear in January. The doctor decided to remove it in day surgery; however, the minor surgery turned out not to be so minor. A biopsy revealed the growth to be squamous cell carcinoma, a very dangerous and aggressive form of skin cancer. Dane was told to go immediately to an oncologist.

Vicki began spending two to three hours every day encouraging Dane and his wife, Diana, with God's covenant promise in Psalm 91. The prognosis from the oncologist/surgeon was grim and frightening. Dane was then sent for a PET scan that showed the cancer had metastasized into the bones in front of and behind his ear. It had also spread to the lymph nodes on the left side of his neck. Surgery was immediately scheduled and two CAT scans were done the day before the surgery. Vicki said she had never interceded so much for one person before Dane. The Lord even woke her in the middle of the night to pray, and He gave her a vision of how He was going to use Dane to touch his church and usher in a fresh outpouring of the Holy Spirit.

On the day of the surgery, Vicki and Diana were permitted to go into a restricted area to pray for Dane. As they prayed, everything came to a complete stop. Even the doctors joined them in prayer. Then, three hours later, one of the doctors came out to share the good news. They had begun the surgery by removing the cancerous growth along with surrounding tissue. The tissue was sent to pathology to make sure they had reached the outer parameters of the unhealthy cells. They also made an incision down the left side of Dane's neck to prepare to remove the lymph nodes along with "all other glands" to insure the disease would be contained.

Can you imagine the surprise of the doctors when the report came back from pathology and the test showed the very dangerous and aggressive skin cancer wasn't squamos at all, but basal cell carcinoma, which very rarely spreads to any other part of the body? The doctors closed Dane's neck and did not remove the lymph nodes.

In addition, the doctor told them that the CAT scans prior to surgery had shown a completely different story from the PET scan the week prior. The first CAT scan indicated there was no cancer in the nodes, so the second scan was done-this one indicating there was no cancer in the nodes or bone! The disease was retreating before their very eyes and by the time they did the surgery, the threat of death had been rebuked by the Lord.

The doctor was confused and kept saying, "I don't know how this happened!" It was all Vicki and Diana could do to keep from just running and praising through the hospital. Dane was supposed to be in the hospital for several days and then have chemo and radiation treatment, but he went home the day after surgery, cancer free. Thank God that, as we know from 2 Corinthians 4:18, "the things which are seen are temporal, but the things which are not seen are eternal."

Nazi Prison Camp

From *Clippings from My
Notebook* by Corrie ten Boom.

Many people came to know and trust the Lord during
World War II. One was an Englishman who was held
in a German prison camp for a long period of time. One
day he read Psalm 91. "Father in heaven," he prayed, "I
see all these men dying around me, one after the other.
Will I also have to die here? I am still young and I very
much want to work in Your kingdom here on earth."

He received this answer: "Rely on what you have
just read and go home!" Trusting in the Lord, he got up
and walked into the corridor toward the gate. A guard
called out, "Prisoner, where are you going?"

"I am under the protection of the Most High," he
replied. The guard came to attention and let him pass,
for Adolf Hitler was known as "the Most High." He
came to the gate, where a group of guards stood. They
commanded him to stop and asked where he was
going. "I am under the protection of the Most High." All

the guards stood at attention as he walked out the gate.

The English officer made his way through the German countryside and eventually reached England, where he told how he had made his escape.

He was the only one to come out of that prison alive.

Sergeant Harold Barclay

This testimony about Sergeant Harold Barclay of Brownwood, Texas, is told by his daughter, Janie Boyd.

Sergeant George Harold Barclay served in World War II in General Patton's 320th Infantry of the U.S. Army, Company E. Continuous fear eliminated any expectation of ever returning to his wife and baby daughter. The same fear kept his wife terrified when she would see a Western Union truck delivering letters of war casualties. Once a Western Union messenger came to her door by mistake and she said that she froze with terror. Sometimes as many as six weeks would go by without a letter, during which time the media reported that half of Harold's company had been killed. The Battle of the Bulge saw his whole outfit cut off from the rest of the army.

Finally, however, a letter came from Harold saying that God had given him Psalm 91, and he now had absolute certainty that he would come home without even an injury. So certain was he of this promise in Psalm 91 that when the medics said they needed volunteers to go to the front lines to bring back the injured, Harold volunteered and made repeated trips under extreme enemy fire, saving many lives.

The citation for the Bronze Star Award that he received said "for bravery," but Harold insisted that it wasn't bravery since he knew nothing would happen to him because of the covenant promise God had given to him in Psalm 91. When he came home without a scratch, it was obvious that angels had indeed borne him up in their hands, allowing no evil to befall him.

John G. Lake

Told by Peggy Joyce Ruth.

I have often read accounts of the time when John G. Lake took fraught from the bubonic plague in his hand and placed it under a microscope, where people watched in amazement as the germs literally died instantly on contact with his hand. I was puzzled for years, wondering what kind of anointing he possessed to bring about that kind of supernatural phenomenon.

Nothing could have pleased me more than when I learned Mr. Lake's secret-his wholehearted belief in the Psalm 91 covenant umbrella of protection that God has provided for all of His children who trust His promise more than they trust in what they see and feel in this world.

On page 340 of the book *John G. Lake: The Complete Collection of His Life Teachings,* Mr. Lake made the statement that confirmed the secret to his supernatural protection: "For many years God kept me so that sickness and death could not touch me, from the day that I saw in the ninety-first Psalm a man's privilege of entering into God, not only for healing, but health and having God and the life of God in every fiber of his being."

Mary Johnson

Mary Johnson lives in
Brownwood, Texas.

After returning from a five-day Red Brangus Cow sale
where my husband and I also met our daughter to
buy clothes for our soon-to-be-birthed first grandchild, I had gotten an early start that morning to catch
up on my chores. We live twelve miles out in the
country, so I was surprised to be interrupted by a
young man in an old van–supposedly lost–asking for
a drink of water.

The pretense was over when he pulled a gun and
told me to get in the car. My surprised scream was
soon stifled when he threatened my life if I did that
again. I was thrown into the back of the van, where a
man wearing a nylon stocking on his head put athlet-
ic tape over my mouth and hands and covered my
head with a black windbreaker. Black shag carpet covered the sides, floor, and roof of the van. The windows
were covered with black curtains.

I couldn't tell where they were taking me. I knew that we crossed railroad tracks and ended up on a gravel road. I had never been so frightened in my life. All I could think about was that I was soon to be fifty—soon to be a grandmother-and I wasn't sure I would live to see either. But my greatest fear was being raped. Finally, however, I came to my senses and started claiming my spiritual covenant promise of protection. I suddenly realized that I was a child of God, fear was of the devil, and God would not let anything happen to me.

By this time we had stopped. With a wool cap pulled down over my face, I was led over a barbed wire fence and across a pasture to an old, abandoned ranch house where I was handcuffed to the bathroom lavatory pipes. One of my kidnappers asked, "What would be the best way to get your husband to cooperate without alerting the police?" Then I was warned that if he went to the police he would never see me again—alive. A phone call with all the usual kidnapping threats and instructions was planned, and then I was left to my dilemma.

Still quoting my promises, singing hymns of deliverance and thanking God, I was frantically working to get the pipes loose, but they wouldn't budge. God said in Psalm 91:15: "In your day of trouble, call upon Me and I will answer." I started praying, "Lord, I am calling on You! I can't do this, but You can. Show me a way to get loose." Then, for the first time, I noticed a tiny pipe coming up the back of the sink. I don't have any idea how I was able to break through, but I know it was a miracle because later the FBI agent couldn't believe I was able to do what I did.

Feeling sure the kidnappers would make their call to Don and be back shortly, I was out the back door and over the fence in no time. I had no idea where I was, but I was confident God would get me where I needed to be. Twelve miles later I came to a house with every door locked except the front door. (I later found out that the owner never left her doors unlocked, except on this particular day.) After several calls, the sheriff was on his way to get me, but my husband had already left for Goldthwaite, Texas, with the ransom money.

The kidnappers skipped that first meeting but called at 12:30 that night with a new appointed place to meet in Austin, Texas. Obviously, they didn't know I had escaped. This time it was the Texas Rangers who met and took the first man into custody; later, the second one was apprehended. I was called to Austin by the FBI to pick him out of a lineup. All I asked was for the men in the lineup to wear a ball cap and say, "Would you get me a glass of water?" With that, I was able to successfully pick him out of the group and my job was over.

I thank God for His covenant of protection in

Psalm 91. We do not have to be afraid of the "terror of what man can do to us—it will not approach us when we run to God and dwell in His shelter."

The man who was convicted of this crime was no amateur criminal. According to police, he had a habitual crime problem since his youth and had previously been convicted and imprisoned for robbery, indecency, and sexual assault. For this present offense he was sentenced to ninety-nine years in prison. The sheriff told Mary Johnson that they had never had anyone in their local jail as malicious as this man. The FBI was shocked that Mary was able to escape and even more shocked that she had not been beaten, raped, or murdered. One of the FBI agents made the comment, "We cannot believe we are sitting here today with you and that you are alive and well." Few people understand the power that is in this wonderful covenant!—Peggy Joyce Ruth

Chris and Ginny Donovan

Ginny Donovan relates a hiking
and camping adventure in
Wyoming's Grand Tetons that she
and her husband will never forget.

As we were breaking camp that Tuesday morning, we
commented on the eight-inch snowdrifts around the
tent–sleet and snow had slammed us during the
night. We packed up and headed toward the North
Fork Cascade Canyon.

It sleeted and snowed nearly nonstop that day.
Although we had on our raingear, it was "wetting out"
where our packs were rubbing constantly. We passed
many day hikers–all headed in the opposite direction-
who gave grim forecasts of the weather: "A cold front
is coming in. It's going to get much worse than this."

After a few minutes of hiking in the deepening
snow, Chris, who was walking several yards behind
me, said, "Here's what we can do. We can spend
tonight in North Fork Cascade Canyon, and then

tomorrow, we'll hike over Paintbrush Divide into Paintbrush Canyon, and then to the truck. We'll finish the trip a day early." Relief washed over me. I looked up at the sky—it was snowing harder now—and said to Chris, "What if we just try to get over the pass today? Could we make it to the truck before dark?"

It was 1:45 in the afternoon. We could see the trail leading up to the divide. It was a continuous line uphill. We looked at the map—we were facing a 1,700-foot elevation gain. We thought we could hike up the pass in about three hours and then go down into the canyon on the other side. We could always spend the night in Upper Paintbrush Canyon if we were too tired to make it back to the truck that afternoon (getting to the truck was about a four-to-five-mile downhill hike).

We decided to go for it. The weather seemed to be letting up a bit, but we knew it would probably get worse. Not wanting to be stranded in a blizzard, we thought it would be best to head up and over the divide. The snow was getting deeper—it was four inches thick now and packing on the top of my boots.

We came to a sign that said, "Paintbrush Divide, 2.4 miles." "Oh shoot," I said. "I didn't think it would be that long!" We had to do it, though—we had to get over it before the really bad weather hit. Chris stopped to get something out of his pack and told me to go ahead. Lord knows I needed a head start. I began trudging through the deep snow up the trail to the divide. I was pacing myself and repeating the mantra, "I can do this. I can do this."

The higher I got, the more frequent breaks I had to take. I was breathing entirely through my mouth because I just couldn't get enough air through my nose. The sun had started to peek through the clouds and the snow stopped. I thanked God for letting us get up the mountain without sleet and snow hitting us in the face. Chris easily caught up to me. We had maybe gone three-quarters of a mile at this point. My legs and lungs were burning. I took a couple of sips from a water bottle and kept trudging along. Chris got in front of me so I could step in his footprints instead of forging my own in now nine-inch-deep snow.

The sky was still clearing. We kept on and came to the shorter, steeper switchbacks. We were probably close to 9,500 feet at this point. My quad muscles felt like they were being scraped with a cheese grater and I just could not get enough air. Chris was having to encourage me now: "Come on, baby–we're almost there. You're doing great–come on–we can do this."

We went on and on. I thought we would just continue climbing into the sky without reaching the top of this blasted mountain. The sky suddenly began to darken and the wind picked back up. Snow was blowing everywhere. I started to feel sleepy and con-fused. *Where were we again?* I stumbled behind Chris and struggled to focus on where his footprints were.

We were close to the top now, and it was an all-out blizzard—complete white-out. We couldn't see any surrounding mountaintops. The trail had disappeared beneath the snow. We saw a sign in the distance and hoped it would point us to the trail but instead it said "Jenny Lake" and pointed down in the direction we had just come from.

Chris noticed some small rocks stacked on larger ones, an indication throughout the park of the trail. We headed that direction. The wind was now blowing at fifty miles an hour. My face was literally frozen, completely covered with ice. I tried to tell Chris, but my lips wouldn't move at first-it felt like I had been stung by a bee. Finally, I got it out: "Chris, my face is frozen." He quickly stopped and dug out my balacla-va (a head, face, and neck covering) which was warm and almost instantly thawed my face.

I followed him some more as we continued to look for the trail which would lead us down into the canyon and out of the wind and snow. Then it hit me: I had hypothermia. My mind flashed back to the page I had read in a medical mountaineering book on the subject: "The person will become very sleepy, disori-ented, and confused. He or she will just want to lay down and go to sleep. Death can/will follow."

I told Chris, "Honey, I have hypothermia," and described my symptoms. He said, "Okay, baby. We've gotta find a place to get out of this wind." We were stumbling around and could barely see. The wind had blown the snow pretty thin in one strip, so we tried to stay there to keep from having to forge through the nearly waist-deep snow on either side. I was shaking violently as my body tried to warm up. Chris kept reaching for me, saying, "Come on sweetie. Come on baby. Stay with me here." I was trying to think of my name but I could not remember it.

Chris asked me to sing him a song. I wanted to sing "Jesus Loves Me" but could only say "Jesus." The part of my brain that knew the lyrics could not communicate with the part that operated my mouth.

We came to another sign that said "Paintbrush Divide, 10,700 feet." I was so mad to see that. I didn't care how high we were-I just wanted to get off that mountain! The next sign was a little more helpful. It said "Paintbrush Canyon" and had an arrow pointing to the left. We were on the right track to hit the trail into the canyon!

The cloud we were in briefly cleared and I got a glimpse of a very steep mountainside. Desperate panic set in. I cried, "Honey, I cannot climb another hill!"

"I know," Chris said. "I have to find a place to put up the tent." I could barely move my feet and couldn't focus on anything. The desire to lie down and go to sleep was so strong. I had to battle it continuously. I knew though that if I lay down, I would likely die. And if I didn't die and only passed out, Chris would have to spend his limited energy to carry me to safety. I was just looking at him, thinking to myself how much I loved and cared for him. I didn't want him to have to drag my limp body around the top of this mountain.

My hands were numb up to my wrists. Part of me was scared to die and said, "No! Keep fighting!" and the other part was exhausted and said, "Just lie down and go to sleep." But I kept looking at my husband who was searching intently for a place to erect the tent. We needed to get warm, and that was what Chris was striving to do.

He found a large rock that had created a little snowdrift wind block. I stood there, utterly helpless, and watched him get out the tent and the stakes and dig through the snow to find the frozen ground in which to drive the stakes. He did the best he could with the tent. Looking back, it's a miracle he was able to do as much as he did.

The icy fingers of hypothermia were beginning to grip Chris's brain, too, but he fought it. He unclipped our sleeping pads, unrolled the sleeping bags, and zipped them together. As he was preparing, he told me to sit down and take off my boots. God was with me. I do not know how, under my own strength, I could have removed those boots. The laces were frozen solid—the knot was frozen too. I vaguely remember moving the laces around the C-clasps to loosen them and pull out my feet. My socks were frozen hard. I expected my toes to be black with frostbite and prepared myself for this, but they weren't. Neither were my hands.

I looked at the thermometer on my fanny pack-it read close to 10 degrees. We had to remove our wet clothes and get in the sleeping bag together. We covered ourselves with the down bags and began shaking so violently that I thought I might get a concussion. Chris held me and kept saying, "I love you, baby. I am so sorry. I love you so much." I was crying, and telling him how much I loved him, too. I kept telling Chris not to let me fall asleep.

I could feel myself starting to warm up again. Chris said, "Oh help us, Jesus!" I chimed in and we started praying together. I plead Psalm 91 over us and called off the spirit of death: "Spirit of death, in the name of Jesus, you must flee. Chris and I are covered by the blood. We are the righteousness of God. You must leave in the name of Jesus!" I asked God to post His angels around our tent: "Keep us safe, Lord. We are Your children."

I was warming up, but when I looked at Chris to tell him, I saw his eyes roll back into his head. The hypothermia had fully set in. "CHRIS!" I screamed. "Chris! No, no, no, baby. You have to stay awake for me. Stay awake, baby. I need you here. I don't want to be in charge! I don't know what to do! Stay awake for me."

"Okay, I will," he said. "Let's just keep talking, keep a conversation going. What do you want to talk about?" I thought it was funny he said that.

"Let's talk about our plan," I said. "How are we going to get out of here?"

"We're going to have to wait until it clears up so we can see the trail and get off of the mountain. But we have to warm up and get our energy back first."

"Okay."

We laid there and continued to shiver. We both smelled so bad, but at the time, I thought Chris smelled wonderful because by stopping to put up the tent when he did, he had saved my life. My hero smelled like stinky armpits, and I loved it.

Another miracle we encountered was that we were at different stages of hypothermia at different times. I had it first, and Chris was able to set up the tent and our sleeping gear. Once I started to warm up, he got it. I was getting better and he was getting worse. His eyes kept rolling back. I told him I needed him. "I need you to stay awake for me, baby."

I looked at Chris's watch and was shocked to see it was 7:15. It would be dark in less than forty-five minutes. I told Chris I had to get dressed and put the waterproof ground covering under us so that our sleeping bags would quit getting on the snow. Most of our gear was strewn on the ground outside of the tent and was covered with snow and ice.

Chris cried, "Oh, Jesus! This was only supposed to be a place to warm up and rest, not a place to spend the night. Oh, Jesus. Please help us."

We were lying on top of large granite rocks. The material on the tent was being whipped about violently in the wind. I prayed that the stakes would not rip from the ground. Chris kept saying, "I feel so loopy–like I'm drugged up or something." I felt the same way. We were both severely dehydrated and my tongue was sticking to the roof of my mouth.

I hauled my pack into the tent and got out my clothes bag. Thank God, Chris had packed everything in waterproof bags. My clothes were all dry. I put on my fleece pants, my rain pants, new socks (dry and warm!), my windproof jacket, and my down jacket and rain parka. My gloves were icy, but I put them on anyway and went out to bring in Chris's bag and our boots, which were now frozen stiff.

With Chris's guidance from inside the tent, I tried to re-stake the front left corner of the tent. I used the trowel to remove eight inches of snow and got a rock to bang the stake into the frozen ground, but I couldn't get it to go in. Chris reached out from under the tent and did it for me. I got back in the tent. Chris had separated the sleeping bags. After the initial life-saving snuggling, we knew we would stay warmer with the bags separated.

Our water was frozen, yet we were so thirsty. Our

fuel was too cold to work, and besides, we were both too exhausted to use the stove. I filled my water bottle with snow, put it in a Ziplock bag, and placed it inside my sleeping bag to defrost. We had to eat something, so I dug out the frozen pita bread and put it in my bag too. I got some clothes for Chris and gave them to him. He was starting to feel a little better as darkness fell. We lay in our bags, completely depleted of energy.

The wind picked up (could it get any harder?!) and the snow was slamming against the tent again. We lay there, holding hands and discussing what we would do in the morning. We prayed that God would make the trail abundantly clear to us and that they sky would be clear so that we could see to make our way safely off of the mountain. We tried to rest a little and nibbled on the pita bread. I ate snow to try to decrease my thirst. Chris put on his headlamp and studied the trail map to determine what we would do in the morning. He said the switchbacks leading off of the mountain were very steep but that we could walk down about two hundred feet and then cut over to the trail.

I didn't sleep much that night, not knowing if we would be able to get off the mountain before the next cold front hit. Thick uncertainty clouded my brain. Would we live? Would we die? No one in the world knew where we were. It was just the Donovans and

God.

I started thinking that if we died, my mom would probably have to clean out our home. I didn't want her to have to go through that. Who would get the pets? Who would find our frozen bodies on the mountain? How would our families react to the news? I had peace about dying because I knew we'd be with Jesus, but I didn't want to die.

I want to have children. I want to be with Chris. I want to paint the house and plant a fall garden and sew and cook and visit friends and listen to music and arrange flowers. I love life! I am so blessed! I just want to live, God–I just want to live!

Trusting God has been one of the biggest issues in my life. After my dad died of brain cancer, I figured it was too risky to completely trust Him for anything "big" again. "He doesn't come through for me when it really counts," I'd told myself.

But on this night, there was nothing left to do but trust Him. And perhaps that's why we were there. When you hold something from God tightly in your fists and keep it from Him, He will be left with no choice but to pry your cold, stiff fingers away. He did that to me. I had a very simple choice to make: trust my Jesus or lay there and panic. I chose God. He spread his wings over our tent that night. The warmth of His blood kept us safe and dry. He did just as He promises He will do in Psalm 91. God, as always, was true to His Word.

I must have fallen asleep, because Chris woke me up at 4:30 and said, "Baby, are those stars I see out there?"

I quickly turned, looked, and shouted, "Praise God! It's clear!"

My heart was soaring. In what seemed to take an eon, the sun finally came up. Chris got completely dressed, putting on every article of clothing he brought, and went over to inspect the trail. The wind was still blowing at close to fifty miles an hour, and the snow was sweeping across the ground. I tried to put on all of my clothes inside of my sleeping bag too, and became completely worn out again. I had to rest for ten minutes.

Chris came back, beaming. He could see the trail "as clear as an interstate." Glory to God–He had answered yet another prayer!!! He is so awesome!

We were relieved, but knew we had to get off the mountain quickly. Standing up outside of the tent, the landscape looked like the moon. Everything was covered in snow and rocks. Huge mountain peaks surrounded us. The sun was coming up and the wind was increasing too. It was hard to keep my balance. I had to get back in my bag to warm up. The snow had melted somewhat in the water bottle, so we shared a few precious sips of water and split a granola bar. I put two frozen energy bars inside my jacket pocket to thaw so we could eat them later. We packed up as quickly as possible. Chris badly separated his thumb-nail from his thumb trying to undo the knots in my frozen shoelaces.

We headed toward the canyon trail. Snow was blowing off the edge of the mountain and swirling upward–it was extremely steep. We couldn't see the beginning of the trail. The first few steps off of the mountain were covered in waist-deep snow. Chris thrust one of his trekking poles into the snow and it went up to the handle. One misstep and we would tumble down the side of the mountain.

We stood there looking at it for a few minutes and decided not to risk it. We were going to go back the way we had come up–the Paintbrush Divide trail. It would add about four miles to our trip to the truck, but it was much safer.

Our footprints from the previous day were covered up, so we tried to remember where we had come up, even though the day before we could not see anything. We found the rocks stacked on top of each other and then–yay!–the Jenny Lake sign! We'd found the trail!

The drifts were knee-to-waist deep. We had wrapped our feet in Ziplock bags to try to keep the snow from wetting our socks again, and it helped. Our toes were blocks of ice, but we were jubilant to be getting down. Chris took a picture of me with my arms in the air, celebrating and praising God for His help and protection.

We talked all the way down the mountain, reliving the previous day and the night. We had hiked uphill for two or three miles on Tuesday going through the North Fork Canyon on the way to the divide. We were hungry, exhausted, dehydrated, and had altitude sickness when we were going up the divide trail. We marveled at how we had the strength to climb the trail. It was beyond strenuous.

Chris said it was a miracle that the stitching on the tent didn't rip—it wasn't designed to withstand those mighty winds. The weather report we'd been given was wrong, and it was part of what had forced us to go up the mountain in the first place. It was warming up outside and some of the snow was starting to melt. The lower we went in elevation, the less snow there was. We were starting to see day hikers now. They asked if we made it across the divide. We told them a brief version of our experience: "We almost died." It sounded too dramatic, but it was true!

We were going back through the North Fork Canyon and would end up at the Jenny Lake boat dock, take a boat ride across the lake, and get a cab ride to Leigh Lake where the truck was parked. It was a long hike, over nine miles, but thankfully downhill. With every step, we were so glad to be alive. We saw a bull moose lying in a meadow. We saw a gorgeous blue sky and tall, strong pine trees. We saw children skipping on the trail with their parents in tow. We were safe. God had brought us through the night. This life...it is a gift indeed. No one guarantees our tomorrows.

We called for a taxi from the Jenny Lake visitor's center. Getting in that Suburban was a luxury. It was soft and warm and moving under its own power, not mine! I was nearly asleep when we came to the truck. We drove to Albertson's, stocked up on all of my favorite shampoos, body washes, and lotions and headed to a hotel to take-hallelujah!–a nice, long, hot shower. I slept like a rock. God is so good.

I can do all things through Him who strengthens me. (Philippians 4:13)

Don Beason

Don Beason is a U.S. Navy World War II veteran (see military testimonies in *Psalm 91: God's Shield*). He sent me this documentation on tornadoes that devastated Grand Island, Nebraska, and then told his unique story of what took place in the midst of that horrible natural disaster.—*Peggy Joyce Ruth*

"Three, possibly four tornadoes grouped together and slashed their way down Bismark Road and South Locust Street. Roger Wakimoto, an assistant for Dr. Fujital of Chicago University, said his preliminary research showed the movement of the tornadoes during the June 3 storm was extremely erratic. According to Wakimoto, it was a very unusual tornado case, seeming to have changed directions moving west down Bismark Road from Knesters Lake and then making a sharp left turn onto South Locust Street. Fujital said the smaller tornadoes began spinning around the larger one and as they began picking up debris, they locked together, forming one large tornado.

"Don Davis, chief meteorologist with the National Weather Service in Grand Rapids, Michigan, said there was a counterclockwise movement of the front. The main tornado came in the second movement and the smaller tornadoes followed behind, creating one of the worst of its kind ever recorded. In all, there were at least seven tornadoes, all going in different directions, but four of them came together to make a large one that did most of the damage."

Interestingly, the tornado at Grand Island was headed directly for Don Beason's office, and the first of the two erratic, unexplainable turns made by the tornado occurred only a few yards before it reached him. It ruined the office directly across the street, but not even a window was cracked in his office.

The second of the two radical changes of direction happened just before the tornado would have swept through Don Beason's farm. The farms next to his were all destroyed. The city map showing the tornado's path confirmed its going straight to his office, then turning in front of his doorstep and going straight for his farm, then once again, turning just short of his property line. The chart dramatically showed the two major surprise changes of direction were directly related to his real estate.

There was no explanation in the natural for the two sudden turns of the tornado-but no one could convince Don Beason it was not the direct result of God's Psalm 91 protection he had been claiming: "I will not be afraid of the destruction (natural disasters) that lay waste at noon."

A few years later, a television station reported a mile-wide tornado heading once again toward Grand Island. Don Beason said, "I went outside and rebuked it and commanded it to turn away and disappear. A minute or two later when I went back into the house, the TV announcer said the tornado had lifted out of sight."

According to Don Beason, it was "more Psalm 91 protection!"

Stella Marshall

Stella Marshall, ninety-five years young, has been satisfied with a long life. She told me her story.
—Peggy Joyce Ruth

I could hardly believe what my eyes were seeing and my ears were hearing as I sat in Stella Marshall's room and listened to her life story. Watching her have no need for glasses or a hearing aid, seeing her walking straight as an arrow, hearing her answer questions with the sharp mind of a twenty-year-old and noticing that she didn't have to take her teeth out at night, I was in awe when Stella told me all about the ninety-fifth birthday party she had enjoyed the day before. (I would have guessed her to be not a day over seventy.)

From the moment I heard some of her fellow church members refer to her as the "Psalm 91 lady," I was determined to get an interview with this beautiful woman. Truly she is the epitome of someone who has been "satisfied with a long life" and "kept safe" by the power of God's promises in Psalm 91.

As a young boy, Stella Marshall's maternal grandfather came by ship to Virginia from Africa, where his own people had sold him and his mother and father as slaves. Stella's mother was one of his eighteen children.

Stella's father, on the other hand, had a much different background. His mother was Irish and it was his sister who later took Stella and her younger brother and sister to rear when their dad died at age twenty-eight after receiving a head injury at the Ennis railroad yard where he worked. Stella, who picked cotton most of her young life, married at sixteen for the sole purpose of never having to pick cotton again, but her dreams of how married life would be did not turn out as she had planned.

She had envisioned having a long table with benches on each side where the family would gather for meals—six boys on one side facing the six girls across from them, and she and her husband sitting at each end of the table. Her idea of how a marriage should be was shattered when it ended in divorce and she was left with three children to rear alone. She had been brought up in a Baptist home, but there was no real relationship with the Lord, so worldliness quickly took hold of her life.

Finally, in desperation, at age fifty-four, Stella

stood by the fence in her front yard and said, "God, You see these cigarettes in my hand? When I smoke these, I'm not going to smoke ever again. I'm not going to take another drink and I'm not going to be with another man as long as I live."

She kept that promise, but for the next five years she could not find satisfaction for the longing and the hungering in her heart for a deeper walk with God. In August 1971, five years after she had given up her flesh life, she asked Jesus into her heart and to be Lord of her life. She was prayed over to receive the baptism of the Holy Spirit and everything in her life changed. She said that each night she would go to sleep and see Jesus standing over her with His hands outstretched.

Before receiving the baptism of the Holy Spirit, Stella had read her Bible with very little understanding. But after being prayed for, Stella said that she was getting something new every time she opened her Bible. Every Full Gospel meeting found Stella on the front row. She couldn't get enough of the Lord.

When I asked Stella why her friends called her the Psalm 91 lady, she said, "When I found Psalm 91, I prayed it over myself and over my family every single day since, and I tell everyone I see about God's wonderful protection."

I was curious how she happened to find it and she told me an interesting story. She was asked to go to Dallas to keep the grandbaby of the fifth-richest man in Texas. The servant's quarters where she lived were secluded, back behind the big mansion. Not being accustomed to staying alone, she began to think about the real possibility of someone breaking into a rich man's property. She got very fearful because she knew that no one would be able to see or hear her if she needed help—so she began crying out to God to take away all her fears.

Faithful to His promises, God supernaturally lead her to Psalm 91, and she has been saying it every day since. Those angels that God placed in charge of her and the confidence that began to build with the knowledge that God had answered her cry grew her faith in God's Psalm 91 covenant of protection. She has been kept from harm from that day forth, and satisfied with a long life.

Stella recalled the time when a flu virus slipped in on her and she began to stand for her healing. When the symptoms didn't leave right away, she said, "Lord, You said if we asked anything, You would do it. I've been expecting my healing. If I haven't heard from You by tomorrow, I am going to the doctor, but my trust is in You." Then she turned over and went to sleep. About 6:30 A.M. Stella said that something woke her up, saying, "You are healed." She said that there was not a place on her that wasn't well. Where she had been struggling to breathe, she could now breathe with ease.

Stella, who has practically raised many of her grandchildren and great-grandchildren, never misses a night praying Psalm 91 over every one of them.

Because of her belief in God and the many blessings He has poured out on her life, Stella wanted to find some way to do something to help others; therefore, in her early sixties, Stella started a routine that lasted over twenty years. She would buy stalks of bananas and distribute them to the residents of nursing homes. She was such a regular visitor that the director of one of the homes scheduled "the banana lady" as an activity all by herself. No matter what the weather, Stella never missed her Thursday afternoon appointment. She never worried if she would have money for her bananas–when Thursday came, the money was always there. For over twelve years, Stella also volunteered at the Casa de Amigos Health Clinic, getting files and signing people in. And all of that is in addition to helping raise her eight grandchildren and thirteen great-grandchildren.

I have often said that just having a lot of birthdays is not always a blessing. It takes a satisfied life to make long life good. You don't have to ask Stella if she is satisfied with her life. Just as obvious as her dissatisfaction with life was before age fifty-four is her satisfaction since then. When I asked her to give me examples of times when she had a problem and God had delivered her after she confessed Psalm 91, she could-n't think of one. I was confused until my husband pointed out the fact that her constant dwelling in the shelter of the Most High had truly sheltered her and picked her up out of the pathway of harm.

Help Your Young Person Overcome His Greatest Fears!

Would you like for your child to know how to overcome the fears that face him? Young people in today's world are faced with so many more worries and uncertainties than those of even a generation ago, but you are not without an answer. *Psalm 91 for Teens* can be one of the greatest gifts you can give to equip your teenager to meet the challenge. Filled with heartwarming stories of young people who have stood on God's Word, this is a book that could easily save his life and the lives of those he loves!

    Psalm 91 for Teens uses the same format as *Psalm 91: God's Umbrella of Protection,* with a similar verse-by-verse look at God's covenant of protection, but it is written on a reading level for youth and filled to overflowing with testimonies, illustrations, a picture album, and application helps to make this truth come alive.

    $8 plus $2 shipping & handling. Call toll free: 1-877-97-books (1-877-972-6657).

Psalm 91: God's Shield of Protection

Military Edition

Psalm 91 has been called the soldier's prayer. Countless soldiers, from the time of the Civil War to those involved in present-day conflicts, have thousands of recorded stories of miraculous interventions. These sixteen short verses carry promise of protection from every evil known to man. This book explaining our Psalm 91 protection covenant needs to be placed in the hands of every member of the military and their families.

Paperback or Hardback
Phone: 325 646-6894
or toll free: (877) 97-BOOKS (877 972-6657)
Paperback: $8.00 + shipping & handling
Hardback: $19.99 + shipping & handling
Special: Add $2 for a Psalm 91 teaching CD.

Is There a Yearning in Your Heart to Trust God More?

Those Who Trust the Lord Shall Not Be Disappointed is a comprehensive study on developing a TRUST that cannot be shaken.

Those Who Trust the Lord Shall Not Be Disappointed has the potential of building a trust in God like nothing you have ever read. Deep down, we direct our disappointments toward God, thinking that somehow He let us down. We trust God for our eternal life; why then can we not trust Him amid the adversities of daily life? Peggy Joyce Ruth has a unique way of showing that victorious living depends upon our unwavering trust in God. She demonstrates with scores of personal experiences just how faithful God really is and details how you can develop that kind of trust which will not disappoint.

Those Who Trust the Lord Shall Not Be Disappointed

$8 plus $2 shipping & handling. Call 325-646-6894 or 1-877-97-books.

Special: Add $2 for a *Those Who Trust the Lord* teaching CD.

Tormented

Tormented: Eight Years and Back is the heartwarming story of a young woman's struggle through eight tormenting years of emotional illness, electrical shock treatments, prescription drugs, and hopelessness—culminating in absolute victory made possible only by God's supernatural delivering power. This book not only describes Peggy Joyce's victorious deliverance, but it also gives step-by-step instructions on how to appropriate deliverance and advice that can guarantee one's steering clear of these demonic forces before they ever have a chance to take hold.

Tormented: Eight Years and Back is not a book just to entertain you. It is one of the most comprehensive books on protection from demonic forces that you will most likely ever read.

$10 plus $2 shipping& handling. Call 325-646-6894 or 1-877-972-6657

Special: Add $2 for a *—Tormented: Eight Years and Back* teaching CD.

If your life is boring… if you yearn for more…this book is for you!

God's Smuggler, Jr.
God has an exciting life for you!
by Angelia Ruth Schum
Peggy Joyce Ruth's daughter

This is the true story of someone who prayed for anything but an average life… "God, never let my life be boring!" You'll be amazed at how God answered that prayer. As the story develops in an exotic place, there is nonstop action with twists and turns as Bibles are smuggled past armed guards into Communist land. This book will challenge you to pray that same prayer without stipulations: "God, please don't ever let my life be boring!"

$8 + $2 shipping &handling. Call 325-646-6894 or 1-877-972-6657.

Psalm 91 Workbook

Make it Meaningful, Make it Real, Make it Mine!

This workbook, based on the work of Peggy Joyce Ruth's examination of Psalm 91 through her book Psalm 91: God's Umbrella of Protection, is the next step designed to seal these truths so deeply within your heart that they will be with you forever.

This Psalm 91 workbook is a concept created to give you a deeper understanding of the protection covenant God has provided for believers, to help you apply Psalm 91 right where you are living and the ability to unlock a personal revelation of these promises It is divided into fifteen lessons.

Each lesson includes applicable parables or analogies to help you think through various life events, questions to initiate personal response to these concepts, fill-in-the-blank questions, and projects to work as a group or as an individual.

$8 + $2 shipping & handling. Call 325-646-6894 or 1-877-972-6657.

Write Your Own Psalm 91 Covenant

I like to make my covenants like a prayer of thanks-giving! For example:

Father, I thank You that You have made it possi-ble for me to dwell in the shelter of You–the Most High. What an awesome privilege. I know I can't dwell in Your presence in my own righteousness–but I come in the righteous blood of Your dear Son, Jesus (v.1). I choose to abide (reside, submit) in Your shad-ow in obedience to You and to Your will (v.1). Lord, You are my refuge and my fortress. You are the God in whom I put my trust. I say it with my mouth and I believe in You and in Your promises with my heart. I have put all my eggs in one basket-and You are the basket. I have no plan B (v.2). I thank You, Lord, that You have promised to deliver me from the snare of the trapper (the enemy). No matter what traps he tries to lay for me, I am safe because I rely on Your deliver-ance (v.3). And I thank You that you deliver Me from the deadly pestilence (deadly diseases–name them!) (v.3). You will cover me with Your feathers and just like a baby bird seeks protection under the wings of its mother, I seek refuge under Your wings. The enemy would literally have to go through You, Lord, to get to me (v.4). I know You will be faithful to Your promises, so Your faithfulness, O Lord, is my shield that I hide behind when the enemy comes to tempt me to fear (v.4).

I know that every extreme evil falls under one of four categories and You have told me not to fear any one of these categories of evil: terror (terrorist attacks or any kind of evil that comes from what another person can do to me); arrows (temptations and attacks of the enemy, strategically aimed at the area where I am most vulnerable); pestilence (deadly diseases, plagues, physical and mental inheritance curses), or destruction (evil that comes through natural disasters over which mankind has no control). Your promise to me is that one thousand may fall at my side and ten thousand may fall at my right hand, but it will not approach me for any purpose. What an awesome promise–I receive it by faith and choose to walk in it (v.5-7). I will only look on with my eyes and see the recompense of the wicked because I have made You, Lord, my refuge (v.8-9). Your promise to me is that no evil will come upon me and no plague or calamity will come against my household. I put the blood covering of Jesus on every member of my household and in Jesus' name I forgive any sins they may have committed (John 20:23, Psalm 91:10). Thank You, Lord, for putting Your angels in charge over me to guard me in all of my ways and to bear me up in their hands lest I strike my foot against a stone (v.11-12). I will take the authority You have given me here and in Luke 10:19

to trample the enemy and his plans under my feet (v.13).

As if these promises were not enough, You have given me seven more bonus promises because I love You and know You intimately by name. Thank You for deliverance. I don't know where I would be today if it were not for Your deliverance from demonic oppression. Thank You for setting me securely on high with You. Thank You that when I call on You, You always answer (1 John 5:14-15). Thank You for being with me when I find myself in trouble and for rescuing me out of that trouble. Thank You for honoring me. You have honored me with Your favor and Your blessings from the day I was conceived. Thank You that You not only give me long life, but a satisfied, long life. And I thank You for allowing me to behold (see and take hold of) Your salvation (health, healing, deliverance, protection, provision) (v.14-16). In Jesus' mighty name, Amen!

Psalm 91
God's Umbrella of Protection

To order additional copies with a credit card call:
Phone: 325-646-6894
or Toll Free: (877) 97-BOOKS (877 972-6657)

or send $8.00* each + shipping & handling to:
The Peggy Joyce Ruth BETTER LIVING Ministries
P.O. Box 1549
Brownwood, TX 76804-1549

*Texas residents, add 6.25% sales tax
Special: Add $2 for a Psalm 91 teaching CD.